Revelation Revealed

After a lifetime of studying the Holy Bible, including commentaries on all of it, I was still no closer to understanding the book of Revelation. Then one day, the Lord opened my mind, and it all became crystal clear...

Michael R. Binder

©COPYRIGHT 2024 Michael R. Binder, M.D.
All Rights Reserved
ISBN: 978-0-9748836-5-6

Saint John the Evangelist: the writing of Apokalypse on Patmos island

Renata Sedmakova / Shutterstock.com

Preface

The Revelation of Jesus Christ is a message that was given to the apostle John from the Creator of the world about the things that would soon come to pass. It is a message of hope to the pure in heart and a message of warning to unbelievers who oppose the Truth. Saint John was to share this message with the growing body of believers and ultimately with the whole world in preparation for the triumphant return of our Lord and Savior Jesus Christ.

In order to properly understand Saint John's vision, let us call to mind a few things about the cultural and political times in which the vision was received. Jesus had recently been crucified and resurrected from the grave. Despite the evidence of this, many Jews remained unwilling to accept Jesus as the promised Messiah. Jesus was a threat to their traditional beliefs, national pride, and family ties. Moreover, clinging to the familiar was much easier than embracing the Lord's dynamic teachings and radical call to love. Also, there was a great deal of risk in becoming a follower of Christ. The Jewish elders had accused Jesus of blasphemy, and, based on rumors that Jesus was a king, Roman authorities considered Jesus and His followers to be a threat to Caesar. This led to the persecution of the early Christians by both Jewish zealots and Roman authorities. During the first several centuries after the resurrection, many of the Lord's followers were arrested, turned over to the Romans, and punished for their beliefs. One of those was the Revelator himself—the apostle John—who received the Revelation while he was exiled on the island of Patmos. What had become very apparent to Saint John during his exile was that the teachings of Jesus were quite contrary to the teachings of the world. This created a spiritual battle that was being played out in the circumstances in which John found himself. Not surprisingly then, much of Saint John's vision makes specific references to the social, political, and religious setting of his time.

Of all the books of the Holy Bible, the book of Revelation has traditionally been the most difficult to interpret because it is so shrouded in Semitic idioms and cultural symbolism. In addition, the chronology of events is difficult to follow because many of the events portrayed are repeated throughout the prophesy without a clear sequence of the events. However, if we read the book of Revelation as a series of visions rather than as one continuous prophesy, the book becomes surprisingly easy to interpret. When decoded in this way, it becomes apparent that there are actually seven prophetic visions, each of which predict the same events unfolding in the same sequence. This crucial observation removes any doubt about the sequence of events in Saint John's prophesy. Decoding the sequence of events is one of the most important parts of interpreting the book of Revelation because it is a prophesy about the things to come.

PRAGUE, CZECH REPUBLIC: The painting of Heart of Jesus in church kostel Svatého Tomáše by unknown artist of 19th century

Renata Sedmakova / Shutterstock.com

Revelation 1:1-4

The Revelation of Jesus Christ, which God gave him to show to his servants the things which must soon come to pass, which he sent and made known by his angel to his servant, John, [2] who bore record to the word of God, and to the testimony of Jesus Christ, about everything that he saw. [3] Blessed is he who reads, and those who hear the words of the prophecy, and keep the things that are written in it, for the time is at hand. [4] John, to the seven churches that are in Asia: Grace to you and peace, from God, who is and who was and who is to come; and from the seven Spirits who are before his throne.

As a preface to revealing what lies ahead, the LORD Jesus gives Saint John a message to pass on to each of the stars of the seven churches in Asia (Rev. 1:20). Here, the word "star" is an idiom for Bishop or Elder of the church. Saint John also refers to the elders as "angels" and to the churches as "candlesticks" (Rev. 1:20). Angels are messengers, and candles bear the light of the Truth that the angels convey.

Revelation 1:5

And from Jesus Christ, the faithful witness, the firstborn of the dead, and the ruler of the kings of the earth. To him who loves us, and washed us from our sins by his blood.

Jesus paid the price for our sins by shedding His blood on the cross. However, we cannot receive this gift unless we trust in Him more than we trust in ourselves. At the hour of death, our conscience will aggressively accuse us of our wrongdoings, and the question will be: who will I defer to? Will I defer to my own conscience, or will I defer to the LORD Jesus? (1 John 3:20-21; 4:17). In the garden of Eden, Adam and Eve listened more to themselves than to God. As a result, they ate the forbidden fruit and died spiritually. Had they trusted in God more than in themselves, they would have obeyed God and found the tree of Life (Rev. 2:7). We too will find the tree of Life if we trust more in God than in ourselves (Rev. 2:7; 22:14).

Revelation 1:6

And he made us kings and priests for God his Father; to him be the glory and the dominion forever and ever. Amen.

We become kings and priests when we give our lives to the King of kings. When we enter into a marriage union with Christ Jesus, everything that is His becomes ours (Luke 15:31).

Revelation 1:7

Behold, he is coming with the clouds, and every eye will see him, including those who pierced him. All the tribes of the earth will mourn over him. Even so, Amen.

We know that when Jesus Christ returns He will appear in the heavens (the sky) with all His angels and saints (Matt. 25:31; Jude 1:14-15; Zech. 14:5). Then "the dead in Christ will rise first" (1 Thess. 4:16-17). The dead in Christ are those who had passed from this life as true believers. They live "in" Christ, and Christ lives "in" them. Immediately after the resurrection of the dead in Christ, "we which are alive and remain;" that is, the faithful who are still living on earth, "shall be caught up together with them in the clouds to meet the LORD in the air." This is the separation of "the sheep from the goats" that Jesus was referring to in Matthew 25:31-33. Note that Saint Paul says nothing here about the resurrection of the dead who are *not* in

The Raising of Jairus' daughter. 1) Le Sainte Bible: Traduction nouvelle selon la Vulgate par Mm. J.-J. Bourasse et P. Janvier. Tours: Alfred Mame et Fils. 2) 1866 3) France 4) Gustave Doré
Ruskpp / shutterstock.com

Christ. That is presumably because they will not be resurrected at the same time as the righteous. Moreover, their resurrection with the righteous would raise a challenging question: where would they go? Would they inhabit the earth? That would seem unlikely because Saint John tells us that they will be "resurrected," which is different than being raised from the dead (John 5:28-29). Those who are raised from the dead eventually die again, whereas those who are resurrected are raised with an imperishable body (1 Cor. 15:42-45). Revelation 20 is the only place in the Bible that makes reference to the time at which the unsaved souls will be resurrected. Verses 11-13 indicate that the damned will be resurrected after the consummation of the New Heaven and the New Earth, which will occur at the end of the tribulation of the last days (Rev. 20:11-13). They will be judged by Jesus Christ and His saints because the saints will have already have been judged. Saint Peter, in his first letter to the Elect, writes, "Judgment must begin at the house of God" (1 Peter 4:17). And Saint Paul, in his first letter to the Colossians, states that the saints will judge the world (1 Col. 6:2). If the saints are to judge the world, they would have to take their places at the judgment seat of Christ before the resurrection of the damned. Thus, it appears that the unsaved departed souls will be resurrected and judged at the same time as those who die in the end-times tribulation.

That is not to say that those who remain in their graves will fail to witness the return of Jesus, for we are told in Revelation 1:7 that "every eye shall see Him, and they also who pierced Him." Assuming that at least some of those who crucified Jesus will not be saved, the only way that they would be able to witness the LORD's return would be from their graves. We know that this is possible because the spirit, which separates from the body at the time of death, has spiritual eyes. This deserves some explanation.

Prior to death, our spiritual eyes depend upon our physical eyes because we are clothed with the flesh. During the corporeal state, our physical eyes act as tiny windows through which our spiritual eyes can see the physical world. However, once the spiritual body separates from the physical body at death, vision, hearing, and other senses are no longer dependent on nor restricted by the physical body (1 Cor. 13:12). Also, consciousness becomes continuous because, once divested of the physical body, the spiritual body receives continuous stimulation from the outside world. Hence, both the saved and the unsaved, whether they are alive or dead when He comes, will witness the return of Jesus Christ (Rom. 14:11). Those who believed in Jesus and were obedient to His teachings will rejoice at His coming, whereas those who rejected Him will mourn over the fact that their time is up and the day of reckoning has arrived.

REVELATION 1:8

I am the Alpha and the Omega, the beginning and the end, says the LORD God, who is and who was and who is to come, the Almighty.

This is Jesus Christ, the Word of God, speaking. He is the "Alpha" (the beginning) and the "Omega" (the end) of all things. He had no beginning and no end; He is everlasting. In the first chapter of the book of Saint John, we read, "In the beginning was the Word, and the Word was with God, and the Word was God" (John 1:1). Jesus Christ always has been the second person of the Triune God; but in the fullness of time, He came down from heaven and was joined to the flesh so that through His life, death, and resurrection, He could reconcile us to God.

Jesus also refers to Himself as the One who is to come because He will return to take His bride, the church, to Himself and to judge the world. This is in contrast to the beast who "was and is not" because his reign on earth will soon come to an end (Rev. 17:11).

PARIS, FRANCE: Christ in Majesty is surrounded by the Virgin Mary, Joan of Arc and St. Michael, mosaic by Luc-Olivier Merson, Basilica of the Sacred Heart of Jesus in Paris

Zvonimir Atletic / Shutterstock.com

Revelation 1:9

I John, your brother and partner in suffering, and in the hope of Jesus Christ, was on the isle that is called Patmos because of the word of God and the testimony of Jesus Christ.

The suffering described here is not a reference to either the great tribulation or the tribulation of the last days but rather tribulation in general, which Saint John and the early church were experiencing due to religious persecution.

Revelation 1:10

I was in the Spirit on the LORD's day, and I heard behind me a great voice, like a trumpet.

The phrase "in the Spirit" means that the human spirit is seeing things through the eyes of the Holy Spirit rather than through the eyes of the human body. Because the person's attention and, in some cases, the person's entire spirit is caught up in the Holy Spirit, the person temporarily loses awareness of his or her physical surroundings. If the spirit actually leaves the physical body, the body might go limp or even appear to be dead during the time of separation. The "LORD's day" refers to Sunday, the day that Jesus Christ was raised from the dead. "A great voice like a trumpet" indicates the importance of the vision Saint John was about to receive.

Revelation 1:11-12

What you see, write in a book and send to the seven churches: to Ephesus, Smyrna, Pergamum, Thyatira, Sardis, Philadelphia, and to Laodicea. [12] I turned to see the voice that spoke to me. Having turned, I saw seven golden candlesticks.

The seven golden candlesticks are the seven churches that were established in Asia Minor (Rev. 1:20).

Revelation 1:13-15

And among the candlesticks was one like a son of man, clothed with a robe reaching down to his feet, and with a golden sash around his chest. [14] His head and his hair were white as wool, like snow. His eyes were like a flame of fire. [15] His feet were like burnished brass, as if they had been refined in a furnace. His voice was like the sound of many waters.

Though Jesus was both the Son of a woman and the Son of God, He generally referred to Himself as the "Son of man" out of humility and to avoid attracting attention to Himself as the Son of God. Hair as white as wool symbolizes Jesus' purity and wisdom; eyes like a flame of fire symbolizes Jesus' burning love and penetrating discernment; feet like burnished brass symbolizes Jesus' walk through the fire of torture and suffering for our sakes; and voice like many waters symbolizes the spirit of truth (the living water) that proceeds from the mouth of Jesus Christ. This description of Jesus is repeated elsewhere in the Bible (Isa. 29:6; 30:30; Dan. 7:9; 10:6).

Revelation 1:16

He had seven stars in his right hand. Out of his mouth proceeded a sharp two-edged sword. His face was like the sun shining in it's strength.

The seven stars are the "angels" (elders) of the seven churches, and the sharp two-edged sword is the word of God that proceeds from the mouth of Jesus. The word of God is referred to as a sword because it divides truth from error, light from darkness, and righteousness from unrighteousness.

Saint John the Evangelist monastery at Patmos island in Greece

Miropink / Shutterstock.com

Revelation 1:17-18

When I saw him, I fell at his feet like a dead man. He laid his right hand on me, saying, Do not be afraid. I am the first and the last. [18] I am he who lives, and was dead; and behold, I am alive forever more. Amen. I have the keys of death and Hades.

Jesus can appear to people in different forms and for different reasons. Generally, the form He takes is suited to the reason for His appearance. In this case, Jesus appears in all of His glory to show John that He is the Almighty Creator of the universe, the eternal God, who has power over life and death, heaven and hell. Hence John, completely awestruck, falls down at His feet.

Revelation 1:19

Write therefore the things which you have seen, and the things which are, and the things which will come to pass.

Saint John is to reduce to writing the visions that the Lord is about to show him in the context of what He has already shown Him during the course of his discipleship.

Revelation 1:20

The mystery of the seven stars which you saw in my right hand, and the seven golden candlesticks. The seven stars are the "angels" (elders) of the seven churches. The seven candlesticks are seven churches.

Jesus is revealing some of the symbolism in Saint John's vision. The phrase "in my right hand" is symbolic of the Lord's sovereignty and care for the angels (leaders) of the seven churches in Asia Minor.

Revelation 2:1

To the angel of the church in Ephesus write: he who holds the seven stars in his right hand, he who walks among the seven golden candlesticks says these things.

Jesus is telling us that He oversees His churches and their leadership. He is present at every church service and to believers wherever they may be.

Revelation 2:2

I know your works, and your toil and perseverance, and that you cannot tolerate evil men, and have tested those who call themselves apostles and are not, and you have found them false.

Jesus is speaking to the head of the church about those who claim to be His followers but who in fact have no interest in serving Him. In contrast, His faithful servants have patiently endured hardship and persecution in loving service to Him.

Revelation 2:3-5

You have perseverance and have endured for my name's sake, and have not grown weary. [4] Nevertheless, I have something against you seeing that you have left your first love. [5] Remember therefore from where you have fallen, and repent, and do the first works; or else I am coming to you swiftly, and will move your candlestick out of its place, unless you repent.

"Left your first love" means that the head of the church in Ephesus had become complacent just as all of us have a tendency to do when things are going well. The Lord was not saying that he had abandoned the faith because vs. 3 tells us that he

Jesus giving the Farewell Discourse to his eleven remaking disciples, from the Maesta by Duccio, 1308-1311

Courtesy of Wikipedia

had endured and not grown weary. Jesus was calling for a revival of passionate service to God and the early church as opposed to just going through the motions.

REVELATION 2:6-7

But this you have, that you hate the works of the Nicolaitans, which I hate also. [7] He who has an ear, let him hear what the Spirit says to the churches. To him who overcomes I will give to eat of the tree of life, which is in the paradise of my God.

Here, Jesus is complementing the church at Ephesus for renouncing what the Nicolaitans were doing. The word "Nicolaitan" is derived from the Greek word *nicos-laos-ton*, which literally means conquest over the laity. What the Nicolaitan bishops and prelates were doing was compelling the laity to do things that they themselves were not doing. Jesus was calling them out on this hypocrisy just as He had done with the Pharisees in Matt. 23:13-36. He was also reminding them of God's grace toward repentant sinners. Just as Adam and Eve died spiritually by disobeying God, we can live spiritually by obeying God.

REVELATION 2:8-9

To the angel of the church in Smyrna write: The first and the last, who was dead, and has come to life says these things: [9] I know your works, and your oppression, and your poverty; but you are rich, and I know the blasphemy of those who say they are Jews, and are not, but are of the synagogue of Satan.

Jesus is instructing John to write to the Bishop of the church in Smyrna to remind him that the LORD sees the hardship that he and his congregation are going through and wants to remind them that though they are poor in material things, they are rich in spiritual things, which is the true wealth. Those that say they are Jews but are not are those who claim to be faithful to God but whose actions speak otherwise. The Jews were God's chosen people; hence, they were expected to obey God's laws and ordinances. But instead of doing that, these Jews felt that they were justified by their heritage alone, for it is written, "Salvation is of the Jews" (John 4:22). Jesus did not accept this as a substitute for obedience to His word. So He calls them liars and says that they are of the "synagogue of Satan." Satan is the father of lies and the master of deception. The Bishop of Smyrna was ultimately martyred.

REVELATION 2:10

Do not be afraid of the things that you will suffer. Behold, the devil is about to throw some of you into prison, that you may be tested; and you will be oppressed for ten days. Be faithful unto death, and I will give you the crown of life.

"The devil will cast some of you into prison" is a metaphorical way of saying that those who oppose God will also oppose His followers. Just as Jesus was persecuted by the unbelievers, so too would His disciples be persecuted by the unbelievers. "Ten days" is not meant to specify an exact period of time. However, it would seem to indicate a relatively short period of time.

REVELATION 2:11

He who has an ear, let him hear what the Spirit says to the churches. He who overcomes will not be harmed by the second death.

The first death is that of the body; the second death is that of the spirit. To "overcome" means to rise above the temptations of the flesh in obedience to

Old Bible and illuminated cross

Triff / Shutterstock.com

God. The word "flesh" is frequently used by Saint Paul to symbolize carnal needs and desires.

REVELATION 2:12-13

To the angel of the church in Pergamum write: He who has the sharp two-edged sword says these things: [13] I know your works and where you dwell, where Satan's throne is. You uphold my name, and did not deny my faith in the days when that witness of mine appeared, that faithful one who was slain among you where Satan dwells.

Jesus sometimes referred to Himself as the one with the "sharp two-edged sword. This was because God's word pierces into the hearts of men to distinguish good intentions from evil intentions, good works from evil ones. In comparison to a dull instrument, a sharp instrument is able to cut with precision, making fine distinctions. The Word of God is able to "cut to the truth," even between soul and spirit, as for example, when Jesus challenged the rich man, who claimed to be following all the commandments, to sell all his possessions and give to the poor. When the rich man found himself unable to do so, he realized that he favored himself more than God and, thus, was not even able to keep the first commandment (Matt. 19:16-23). A "two-edged sword" can also refer to the fact that God's word applies to ourselves as much as it does to others. Hence, in pointing out someone else's flaws, we are also pointing out our own flaws.

Jesus, the one with the sharp two-edged sword, is instructing John to write to the Bishop in Pergamum to let him know that He is aware of the challenges he is facing there with pagan worshipers and that he recognizes his faithfulness. "Where Satan dwells" is a metaphorical way of saying, land of the heathens. According to church tradition, Bishop Antipas was seized by idol worshippers who were told by demons that they were not able to live in that place on account of Anipas. Saint Antipas was martyred by being burned in a brazen bull-shaped alter during the reign of Roman emperor Nero.

REVELATION 2:14

But I have a few things against you because you have there those who hold the teaching of Balaam, who taught Balak to cast a stumbling block before the children of Israel, to eat things sacrificed to idols, and to commit sexual immorality.

Baal was a false prophet, who taught that sexuality was a matter of free choice without any moral boundaries. Baal worship caused twenty-four thousand Jews to die of sexually transmitted disease (Num. 25:9; 1Cor.10:8).

REVELATION 2:15-16

And you also have among you those who hold to the teaching of the Nicolaitans. [16] Repent therefore, or else I will come to you quickly, and I will make war against them with the sword of my mouth.

The Nicolaitan leadership was behaving as hypocrites. Jesus warns that He will confront them through one of his faithful servants.

REVELATION 2:17

He who has an ear, let him hear what the Spirit says to the churches. To him who overcomes I will give of the hidden manna, and I will give him a white stone, and on the stone a new name written, which no one knows but he who receives it.

The "hidden manna" is the body of Christ—the Eucharist. A "white stone" is a sign of trust. During

*Jesus the Good Shepherd, Grace Church Chiangmai, Thailand, from the mid 19th century
Reproduction of original Bernhard Plockhorst painting*

Freedom Studio / Shutterstock.com

biblical times, it was a coin-like form of identification made of baked white clay. Pressed into the clay was the seal of the master or a secret name known only to the parties in the transaction. The color white, as used here, is symbolic of the purity that is so prized by God. A "new name" symbolizes one's new life in Christ. Jesus gave Simon Bar-Jonah the new name "Peter" (the rock), and He gave Saul of Tarsus the new name "Paul" (meaning small or humble) after he called him to preach the Gospel. Those who die in Christ may be given a new name upon their entry into the kingdom of heaven.

REVELATION 2:18-20

To the angel of the church in Thyatira write: The Son of God, who has eyes like a flame of fire, and feet like burnished brass, says these things: [19] I know your works, your love, your faith, your service, your patient endurance, and that your last works are more than the first. [20] But I have this against you, that you allowed that woman of yours, Jezebel, who calls herself a prophetess, to teach and to seduce my servants to eat things sacrificed to idols and to commit sexual immorality.

"Eyes like a flame of fire" refers to the LORD's burning love for us. "Feet like burning brass refers to the deep suffering He endured for our salvation. Jesus is praising the church in Thyatira for their good works, but He is also upbraiding them for partnering with Jezebel, who represents sexual immorality and idolatry. Jezebel is recounted in 1 Kings and 2 Kings as an enemy of the prophets and a worshiper of the God of Baal and the goddess Asherah.

REVELATION 2:21-23

I gave her time to repent, but she did not repent of her sexual immorality. [22] Behold, I will throw her into a sick bed, and those who commit sexual immorality with her will I throw into great oppression unless they repent of their works. [23] I will smite her children with death, and all the churches will know that I am he who searches the minds and hearts. And I will give to each one of you according to your deeds.

Here we are warned that God punishes sin unless we make an effort to turn away from it. Some of this punishment occurs as a natural consequence of sin, and some of it is meted out by God to help us recognize the sin. True repentance means more than just apologizing to God; it means turning to God in an effort to change our ways. Unless we repent of ours sins and accept the LORD's atoning sacrifice for them, we will suffer their eternal consequences.

Some have argued that eternal suffering seems unfairly punitive for sins committed in finite time. What we must remember, however, is that sins are spiritual, and spiritual things have eternal consequences. Another way of understanding eternal consequences is to recognize that the spiritual world exists outside of time. It is the eternal present; hence, there could be no "end" to the suffering we experience in the hereafter. In contrast to the natural consequences of sin, the "punishment" that God metes out during our life on earth is actually discipline. Its purpose is to help us become aware of the errors in thinking and behaving that rob us of love, joy, and peace. If the stain of these errors is not removed by accepting the Lord's atoning sacrifice on the cross and prevented by ongoing efforts to live in obedience to God, then we will reap the eternal consequences of our errors.

REVELATION 2:24

But to the rest of you in Thyatira, as many as do not follow this teaching, who do not know, as they say, the deep things of Satan; to you I say that I will not put upon you another burden.

The Transfiguration of Our Lord, Russian icon from the Holy Theotokos Dormition Church on the Volotovo field near Novgorod

Courtesy of Wikipedia

The LORD says that He is satisfied with the commitment of those in Thyatira who were faithful in holding themselves back from idolatry and sexual immorality.

REVELATION 2:25-28

Hold fast to that which you have until I come. [26] He who overcomes, and keeps my works to the end, to him I will give authority over the nations. [27] He will shepherd them with a rod of iron, and mould them like the clay of a potter; as I also was disciplined by my Father. [28] And I will give him the morning star.

We have to remain faithful to the end, not just for one phase of our lives (Rev. 3:10-11). Those who dedicate their lives to God will be molded by God and brought to humility so that they can be of greater service to God and man. During his early years, Moses lived a life of privilege, but the pride that it engendered caused him to get ahead of God's plans for his life and attempt to take matters into his own hands. Thus, he killed an Egyptian in pursuit of justice (Exodus 2:11-12). Then, after wandering in the desert for forty years, he acquired the humility that would allow him to deliver the Hebrew slaves out of the hand of Pharaoh by serving God obediently. Likewise, when God came to the aid of the French during the Hundred Years War with England, he did not work through a well-trained knight; instead, He chose an illiterate girl from a peasant farm—a young maid who, because of her humility, was able to help her people through strict obedience to God. Of course, there is no greater example of humility than Jesus Christ who, despite being equal to God, made Himself of no reputation and went like a lamb to the slaughter for all of us. Thus, if the LORD allows us to experience discipline, suffering, and humiliation, it is only to prepare us for greater service to God and man. The morning star represents the glorious victory over sin and death that God will give to His faithful servants.

REVELATION 2:29

He who has an ear, let him hear what the Spirit says to the churches.

"He who has an ear" is an idiomatic expression that means, "he who is willing to listen." The "spirit" refers to the Holy Spirit, who is the teacher of all truth. Hence, this verse is a call to those who seek the truth.

REVELATION 3:1-2

And to the angel of the church in Sardis write: He who has the seven Spirits of God and the seven stars says these things: I know your works, that you have a reputation of being alive, yet you are dead. [2] Wake up, and hold fast to the things that remain, which you are ready to throw away; for I have not found your works to be perfect before God.

You are respected by people but are in fact lacking in faith and good works.

REVELATION 3:3

Remember, therefore, what you have received and heard; keep it, and repent. If, therefore, you do not watch, I will come as a thief, and you will not know what hour I will come upon you.

The LORD will call us into account when we least expect. In a more general sense, Jesus warns that none of us knows the day or hour of our death; however, when that time comes, we will have to answer for the way we lived our lives (2 Cor. 5:8). This is also a reference to the words of John the Baptist, who warned that the axe is at the foot of the tree. Every tree that does not bear fruit will be cut down and thrown into the fire (Matt. 3:10).

The Devil depicted in the Temptation of Christ, by Ary Scheffer, 1854
Courtesy of Wikipedia

Revelation 3:4-6

Nevertheless, you have a few names in Sardis who have not defiled their garments. They will walk with me in white, for they are worthy. [5] He who overcomes will be arrayed in white robes, and I will not blot his name out of the book of life, but I will confess his name before my Father and before his angels. [6] He who has an ear, let him hear what the Spirit says to the churches.

White is symbolic of purity, and to overcome is to remain faithful to the end. Thus, those who remain faithful to the end will walk with the LORD in white garments. Just as they honored the LORD before men, the LORD will honor them before God.

Revelation 3:7-8

To the angel of the church in Philadelphia write: these things says he who is the holy one; he who is holy; he who is true; he who has the key of David; he who opens and no man can shut, and who shuts and no man can open, says these things: [8] I know your works and behold, I have set before you an open door, which no man can shut, for you have but little power, and yet you have kept my word and have not denied my name.

"Key of David" is a reference to the LORD's ultimate authority over all things. Just as King David held the keys to the city, Jesus holds the keys to life. Any door He opens, no man can shut; and any door He shuts, no man can open. The LORD is the door to our salvation; there is no way to the Father except through Him (John 14:6). Also, the LORD oversees and protects the work He gives us on earth. Without Him, our works are in vain.

Revelation 3:9

Behold, I turn over to the synagogue of Satan, those who say they are Jews, and they are not, but lie. Behold, I will make them to come and worship before your feet, and to know that I have loved you.

A true Jew would keep the commandments and submit to the Truth that had come into the world, but these Jews were doing neither. Instead, they were thinking proudly, assuming that they could trust in the promises God made to their forefathers Abraham, Isaac, and Jacob. Saint Luke tells us that Jesus confronted them about this (Luke 3:8). True believers receive so many blessings from God that their adversaries are eventually put to shame.

Revelation 3:10

Because you kept my command to endure, I also will keep you from the hour of testing, which is to come upon the whole world, to test those who dwell on the earth.

This verse contains three promises. First, it is the LORD's assurance that He will not allow the faithful to suffer more than He permits, and perhaps less than the unfaithful. Second, it is the LORD's promise that He will protect the faithful from the assaults of conscience at the hour of death. Third, it is our first clear indicator that the rapture of the church will occur before the start of the tribulation of the last days.

Revelation 3:11

Behold, I am coming soon. Hold firmly to that fast which you have, so that no man takes away your crown.

We are assured that we must endure but a little while and not allow anyone or anything get in the way of our salvation.

Laodikeia Ancient City, Denizli - Turkey
Klenger / Shutterstock.com

Revelation 3:12-13

He who overcomes I will make a pillar in the temple of my God, and he will not go out again. I will write on him the name of my God, and the name of the city of my God, the new Jerusalem, which comes down out of heaven from my God, and I will write upon him my new name. [13] He who has an ear, let him hear what the Spirit says to the churches.

To make a "pillar" means to firmly establish. That he shall "not go out again" means that those who overcome will no longer experience any pain, sorrow, or suffering. To "write upon him" means to establish in him or assign to him. The Holy Spirit establishes the Spirit of God in our hearts and the word of God in our minds. In Rev. 14:1 we read, "And I looked, and, lo, a Lamb stood on the mount Sion, and with an hundred forty and four thousand, having his Father's name written in their foreheads" (Rev. 14:1). To "write in their foreheads" means to establish the word in their minds. Anatomically, the neural correlates of the mind are carried out by the front part, or "frontal lobe" of the brain, which is located just inside the forehead. To "write on him the name of the city of my God" (vs. 12) means to establish him in the city of God. Also, God literally assigns a new name to those who He establishes in His kingdom.

Revelation 3:14

To the angel of the church in Laodicea write: These things says the Amen; the faithful and true witness; the beginning of God's creation.

Here, Jesus refers to Himself as both LORD and Creator.

Revelation 3:15

I know your works, that you are neither cold nor hot. I wish that you were cold or hot.

"Neither cold nor hot" refers to those in the early church who were religiously-minded but not really committed to Christ. That is, they were "lukewarm." They were talking the talk but not really walking the walk. They were treading the dangerous waters of believing that they were pleasing to God because, in the eyes of others, they appeared to be pleasing to God. This is even more perilous than being an unbeliever because it leads one to believe that there is no need to repent. Jesus said, "No man can serve two masters: either he will hate the one and love the other; or else he will hold to the one, and despise the other" (Matt. 6:24). We cannot be attached to worldly things and be fully surrendered to God at the same time. Nor should we allow ourselves to be swayed by the glory bestowed upon us by people. Rather, we should repent, for in so doing we will lead others to repent and remain true to ourselves.

Revelation 3:16

So because you are lukewarm, and neither cold nor hot, I will vomit you out of my mouth.

Again, to be "lukewarm" is to lack full commitment. Jesus is confronting the church in Laodicea for failing to make a full commitment to God. Jesus wants us to be fully committed to Him so that we can receive His best. The soul that is attached to worldly things has no room for heavenly things. By keeping our eyes focused on God, we protect ourselves from becoming lost in worldly pursuits. Jesus told His disciples, "No servant can serve two masters: for either he will hate the one, and love the other; or else he will hold to the one, and despise the other. Ye cannot serve God and mammon" (Matt. 6:24; Luke 16:13).

The fresco of St. John the Evangelist in cupola of Church Chiesa di Santo Tommaso by C. Secchi from bechin of 20th century

Sedmakova / Shutterstock.com

Revelation 3:17-19

You say, I am rich, and have gotten riches, and have need of nothing. Yet you do not know that you are miserable, and wretched, and poor, and blind, and naked. [18] I tell you to buy from me gold refined by fire, that you may become rich; and white garments, that you may clothe yourself, and that the shame of your nakedness be not revealed; and eye salve to anoint your eyes, that you may see. [19] As many as I love, I reprove and chasten. Be zealous therefore, and repent.

Jesus is confronting the members of the church for placing their confidence in wealth rather than obedience to God. He is calling for repentance, reminding them that He chastens whom He loves (Heb. 12:6).

Revelation 3:20

Behold, I stand at the door and knock. If anyone hears my voice and opens the door, I will come in to him, and will sup with him, and he with me.

Jesus knocks on the door of every person's heart. He does this in various ways. Sometimes He does it through His counsels, sometimes through unlikely coincidences, sometimes through signs and wonders, and sometimes through direct revelation. These are invitations from the LORD. However, it is up to us to accept the LORD's invitation. The frightening thing is that the LORD will not force us to accept Him. The reason He will not force us is that even a good thing is perceived as evil if it is enacted by force. That's frightening because without the LORD Jesus, we are nothing, we can do nothing, and we can become nothing (John 15:5).

Revelation 3:21-22

To him who overcomes, I will give to sit down with me on my throne, even as I overcame, and sat down with my Father on his throne. [22] He who has an ear, let him hear what the Spirit says to the churches.

Jesus told His disciples that those who followed Him faithfully would, like Jesus, sit on thrones to judge the twelve tribes of Israel (Matt. 19:28; Luke 12:30).

The First Prophetic Vision

Revelation 4:1

After these things, I looked and saw a door opened in heaven, and the first voice that I heard, like a trumpet speaking to me, was one saying, Come up here, and I will show you the things that must soon come to pass.

Historically, trumpets were used to call attention to events of great importance. Hence the phrase, "Like a trumpet" is used to indicate that a very important message is about to be conveyed. The phrase, "Come up here" indicates that Saint John's soul is being drawn out of his physical body and into the spiritual realm so as to allow him to fully attend to what the LORD is communicating to him.

Here begins the first of seven prophetic visions, each of which describes the events to come in the same chronological order. Furthermore, both the events and the sequence in which they occur are consistent with other parts of the Bible. This is important to note because the consistency allows us to verify the order of the events. Once we

Mosaic of the twenty-four elders from the Book of Revelation, Santa Prassede, Rome, Italy
Stig Alenas / Shutterstock.com

see the book of Revelation as seven separate visions, there can be no debate about the sequence of the events portrayed.

REVELATION 4:2-3

Immediately I was in the Spirit. Behold, there was a throne set in heaven, and one sitting on the throne. [3] The one who sat looked like a stone of jasper and sardonyx, and round about the thrown was a rainbow, like an emerald to look at.

In this first prophetic vision, we are given a picture of the thrown of God. The One on the throne is the LORD Jesus Christ. The rainbow about the thrown is symbolic of hope, deliverance, and the promises of Christ. In Genesis, chapter 9, the LORD God told Noah that He would "set His bow in the cloud" as a symbol of His promise to man and to every living creature that the earth would never again be flooded to destroy all flesh (Gen, 9:3).

REVELATION 4:4

And around the throne were twenty-four seats. And on the seats were twenty-four elders sitting, dressed in white garments, with crowns of gold on their heads.

Gathered around the throne of God are those faithful servants who are part of the first resurrection. The small number of them (though the exact number should not be taken literally) tells us that they are a very select group. They are the LORD's most faithful servants—the martyrs. Included among them are not only those who were literally decapitated in the name of the LORD; a martyr is any person who fully surrenders his or her life to God. When we fully surrender to God, we allow our heads to be cut off in the sense that we exchange our own way of thinking for a new way of thinking—the LORD's way of thinking.

Accordingly, the number twenty-four also represents the twelve tribes of Isreal and the twelve Apostles, who are symbolic of the LORD's teaching in the Old and New Testaments of the Bible.

We know that the elders were with God at the time of Saint John's vision because the evangelist was told that the remainder of the vision pertained to the "things which must be hereafter." That is, subsequent to the time of the vision (Rev. 4:1). Saint John saw the elders gathered around the altar at the start of the vision, before he saw the events that were to come.

That God would raise His most faithful servants in advance of the rest of the believers is consistent with the fact that He raised Jesus, His most faithful servant, in advance of His other servants. It also implies that the elders who Saint John saw were received into heaven sometime between the resurrection of Jesus and the time that he received the vision. It would seem that more elders are being added to their number as we await the general resurrection at the second coming of Christ.

REVELATION 4:5-8

Out of the throne proceed lightnings, sounds, and thunders. And there were seven lamps of fire burning before his throne, which are the seven Spirits of God. [6] And before the throne was a sea of glass that looked like crystal; and in the middle of the throne, and around about it were four living creatures full of eyes before and behind. [7] The first creature was like a lion, and the second was like a calf, and the third had the face of a man, and the fourth was like a flying eagle. [8] The four living creatures, each one of them having six wings, are full of eyes within. They have no rest day and night, saying, Holy, holy, holy is the LORD God Almighty, who was, and who is, and who is to come!

Old painting of Jesus Christ in The Holy Monastery of the Great Meteoron, Greece
Ollirg / Shutterstock.com

"Lightnings, sounds, and thunders" denote God's glory and the power of that which proceeds from the thrown of God. From His thrown proceed love, wisdom, and guidance to help us during our time of testing and spiritual growth on earth. The four living creatures full of eyes depict the omniscience of God and the manifold gifts that He gives His servants (Rev. 4:6-8). That they have "eyes before and behind" is a reference to God's ability to see both the past and future. It was through these eyes that the prophets were able to see into the future and look into the hearts of men. The lion is symbolic of strength, the calf is symbolic of sacrifice, the man is symbolic of intelligence, and the eagle is symbolic of omnipresence. The four living creatures are similar to the ones described by the prophet Ezekiel (Ezk. 1:5-12) and the same as those that Isaiah saw in his vision (Isa. 6:1-6).

These symbols were used by God because in the biblical days rulers had lions and leopards near their thrones. In Daniel 6:7 we are told that the king of Ethiopia had lions in his palace. Also, in Rev. 5:6 we see the LORD Jesus Christ described as a Lamb in the midst of the elders, having seven horns and seven eyes. This kind of symbolism helped the people understand God in earthly terms. The seven spirits of God are the seven gifts of the Holy Spirit; namely, wisdom, understanding, knowledge, counsel, fortitude, piety, and fear of the LORD (Acts 2:3). A similar reference is made in Rev. 5:6. "Which was, and is, and is to come" represents God's eternal sovereignty as opposed to the temporary reign of the beast, who is described in Rev. 17:11 as the one who "was, and is not."

REVELATION 4:9-11

When the living creatures give glory, honor, and thanks to him who sits on the throne, to him who lives forever and ever, [10] The twenty-four elders fall down before him who sits on the throne, and worship him who lives forever and ever, and throw their crowns before the throne, saying, [11] Worthy are you, our LORD and our God, the Holy One, to receive glory, honor, and power, for you created all things, and because of you they are, and came into existence.

The LORD will be praised forever and ever.

REVELATION 5:1-6

On the right hand of him who sat on the throne I saw a book written inside and out. It was sealed with seven seals. [2] Then I saw a mighty angel proclaiming with a loud voice, Who is worthy to open the book, and to break its seals? [3] No one in heaven above, or on the earth, or under the earth, was able to open the book, or to look upon it. [4] And I wept much, because no man was found worthy to open the book, or to look upon it. [5] But one of the elders said to me, Do not weep. Behold, the Lion who is of the tribe of Judah, the Root of David, has overcome; he is worthy to open the book and its seven seals. [6] And I beheld in the midst of the throne and of the four living creatures, and in the midst of the elders, a Lamb standing, as it had been slain, having seven horns, and seven eyes, which are the seven Spirits of God sent out into all the earth.

Now Saint John sees the history and future of the spiritual battle that has been waged on earth since the day that God created humankind. This deserves some explanation. When God formed man out of the dust of the ground and breathed into his nostrils the breath of life, He animated the physical body (dust of the earth) with a spiritual body (breath of God). The head of the spiritual

Ancient Pool of Bethesda ruins. Old City of Jerusalem, Israel

Shujaa_777 / Shutterstock.com

body is called the "mind" and the head of the physical body is called the "brain." During our life on earth, the mind and the brain are continually interacting in the familiar process that we call "thinking."

The spiritual body has two distinct functions and, correspondingly, two distinct natures: it has a carnal nature, and it has a moral nature. Its carnal nature is characterized by carnal instincts that help ensure our survival in the flesh. These include the perception of pain, temperature, touch, hunger, fatigue, and a variety of other sensations that help ensure our physical well-being. The emotions that these sensations produce, some of which are pleasant and others of which are unpleasant, are also part of our carnal nature. Our moral nature is characterized by moral instincts that help us grow spiritually and survive as a society. These include honesty, patience, kindness, charity, forgiveness, and other virtues that, when practiced through the gift of will, form the basis of love. Our moral nature gives rise to the feelings of peace, joy, shame, and guilt, all of which are in the service of our moral instincts, just as our carnal emotions are in the service of our carnal instincts.

In terms of attributes then, we have two minds, two fundamentally different aspects of our being. The carnal mind corresponds to our carnal nature and thinks about things practically, while the moral mind corresponds to our moral nature and thinks about things ethically. When the carnal mind and the moral mind are satisfied and in agreement, the mind is at ease, and the soul is at peace. However, when circumstances arise that bring the carnal mind into conflict with the moral mind, the mind experiences intrapsychic tension. This phenomenon became the focus of an entire school of psychoanalysis pioneered by the renowned Austrian neurologist Sigmund Freud. It is also the root of the battle between good and evil that began in the garden of Eden and culminates in Saint John's revelation.

This revelation is unveiled in terms of a book that is held in God's hand, having seven seals. Jesus Christ, who is described as the Lion of the tribe of Judah (vs. 5), is the only one who is worthy to open the book, for He is the only one who was able to overcome all the temptations of the flesh. Temptations of the flesh are thoughts, experiences, and circumstances that force us to choose between our carnal mind and our moral mind. We overcome temptation whenever we forgo our carnal desires in an effort to honor our moral responsibilities. Here Jesus, the One who overcame, is depicted as a lamb who had been slain, having seven horns and seven eyes, which we are told represent "the seven spirits of God sent forth into all the earth" (Rev. 5:6). The seven spirits are the seven gifts of the Holy Spirit. The reference here is to the prophet Joel, who wrote, "And it shall come to pass that I will pour out my spirit onto all flesh" (Joel 2:28-29; Acts 2:17-19). We receive the Holy Spirit when we surrender our lives to God.

REVELATION 5:7-8

And he took the book out of the right hand of him who sat on the throne. [8] And as he took the book, the four living creatures and the twenty-four elders fell down before him, each one having a harp, and golden bowls full of incense, which are the prayers of the saints.

Jesus Christ, the Lamb of God, our LORD and Savior, is the only one who was worthy to take the book out of the right hand of God the Father, the One who sits on the throne. The four and twenty elders are those who are part of the first resurrection referred to again in Rev. 20:6. The prayers of the saints are those that are conveyed to God by the saints and answered by God through the saints.

REVELATION 5:9

They sang a new song, saying, You are worthy to take the book, and to open its

Mosaic of Jesus Christ at Hagia Sofia, Istanbul
Muharremz / Shutterstock.com

seals: for you were slain, and redeemed us for God with your blood, out of every tribe, language, people, and nation.

The redeemed will come from all walks of life; they will come from all nations, tongues, and religions. Salvation does not depend on one's ethnic or religious background but on repentance and surrender of one's own will to God's will in Christ Jesus. In speaking to the Jews, Jesus said, "Other sheep I have, which are not of this fold: them also I must bring, and they shall hear my voice; and there shall be one fold, and one shepherd" (John 10:16). Whoever surrenders his or her life to Christ leaves the physical world spiritually and becomes a citizen of heaven.

REVELATION 5:10

And have made us kings and priests for our God, and we will reign on the earth.

Those who receive the Holy Spirit become co-heirs with Christ. They reign on earth through the wisdom and power of the Spirit, which is not limited by logic and experience.

REVELATION 5:11-12

I looked, and I heard as it were the voice of many angels around the throne, and the living creatures, and the elders; and the number of them was ten thousands of ten thousands, and thousands of thousands; [12] saying with a loud voice, Worthy is the Lamb who has been slain to receive the power, wealth, wisdom, strength, honor, glory, and blessing!

This verse reiterates the idea that the number of souls who are part of the first resurrection is far greater than the twenty-four referenced symbolically in Rev. 5:8. All of these elders or "big saints" are gathered around the throne praising and glorifying God for their salvation.

REVELATION 5:13-14

And I heard every created thing which is in heaven, on the earth, under the earth, in the sea, and everything that is in them, saying, To him who sits on the throne, and to the Lamb be blessing, and honor, and glory, and dominion forever and ever. [14] And the four living creatures said, Amen. And the twenty-four elders fell down and worshiped him who lives forever and ever.

The entire creation gives glory to God, for He is the Creator of all that is seen and unseen (Ps. 19:1). The fact that the dead can see the glory of God and hear His praises is consistent with the idea that those who crucified Jesus will see Him coming on the clouds of glory even if they are still in their graves (Rev. 1:7).

REVELATION 6:1-11

I saw that the Lamb opened one of the seven seals, and I heard one of the four living creatures saying, as with a voice of thunder, Come and see. [2] And I looked and saw a white horse, and he who sat on it had a bow, and a crown was given to him; and he went forth conquering, and to conquer. [3] And when he opened the second seal, I heard the second living creature saying, Come and see. [4] And I looked and saw a red horse. And to him who sat on it was given power to take peace from the earth, and that they should kill one another; and there was given to him a great sword. [5] And when he opened the third seal, I heard

*Old illustration of Saint Sebastian martyrdom
created by Pecher, published on L'Illustration Journal Universel, Paris, 1857*

Marzolino / Shutterstock.com

the third living creature saying, Come and see. And behold, a black horse, and he who sat on it had a balance in his hand. [6] And I heard a voice in the middle of the four living creatures saying, A measure of wheat for a denarius, and three measures of barley for a denarius. And see that you do not damage the oil and the wine. [7] And when he opened the fourth seal, I heard the fourth living creature saying, Come and see. [8] And behold, a pale horse, and he who sat on it, his name was Death, and Hades followed him. And power was given to them over one-fourth of the earth, to kill with the sword, with famine, with death, and with the wild animals of the earth. [9] And when he opened the fifth seal, I saw under the altar the souls of those who had been slain for the Word of God, and for the testimony of the Lamb. [10] And they cried with a loud voice, saying, How long, Master, the holy and true, until you judge and avenge our blood on those who dwell on the earth? [11] And a long white robe was given to each of them; and they were told that they should rest yet for a little while, until their fellow servants and their brothers, who would also be slain as they were, should complete their course.

With the opening of the first seal we are given an image of Jesus Christ as a glorious rider on a white horse. In the East, white horses are rare and are normally owned by kings, princes, and noblemen. A white horse and a crown stand for princely authority and ultimate victory. The Son of God is going out to conquer sin, death, and the forces of evil on earth.

With the opening of the second seal we are introduced to the adversary, here depicted as a red horse whose rider has a sword. The color red and the sword symbolize death and destruction, the era of persecution of the church. During the first 250 years of Christianity, the church came under heavy attack. Millions of Christians were martyred under the direction of Roman authorities.

The opening of the third seal (vs. 5) reveals a black horse whose rider has a balance in his hand. This depicts the era of heresies that threatened to take away the sound doctrine of the orthodox church. The balance scales symbolize the need to carefully weigh the different teachings and to cling to that which was grounded in justice and love. Regardless of these threats, the oil and the wine, which symbolize the sacraments of the church, were to be preserved.

The opening of the fourth seal reveals a pale horse, which depicts all the tribulations of the world, including the persecution of the early church, and the physical death that followed from it.

With the opening of the fifth seal (vs. 9) we see the martyrs under the altar of God dressed in white robes. They are under the alter because they gave their lives for Jesus Christ, who, as LORD over them, was slain on the alter of sacrifice. In giving their lives to Christ, they had been washed by His sacrificial blood, which streams down upon them from the alter of sacrifice. They are crying out for justice on earth and for retribution upon those who wrong the innocent. Until Christ returns, the world will continue to be under God's grace. But when the LORD returns, justice will be served (Rev. 22:12).

Here we also see the chronology expressed in the first prophetic vision. From verse 6:11, we know that the rapture of the church has not yet occurred because the elders under the altar are told to wait patiently until their brethren also bear witness to the Truth. Specifically, this places us in the period of time between the resurrection of Jesus and the rapture of the church. In Rev. 20:6 we will see that the elders under the altar have already been resurrected. Some were resurrected

Wall relief on arch of titus depicting Menorah taken from temple in Jerusalem in 70 AD - Israel history, Jewish war

Graceenee / Shutterstock.com

with Jesus (Matt. 27:52), and others were resurrected later. They are again referenced in Rev. 5:3, 5:5, 5:6, 5:8-14, and 6:9-11.

With the opening of the sixth seal, we see the start of the tribulation of the last days, which Jesus warned would occur immediately after the "tribulation of those days" (Matt. 24:29). The tribulation of "those days" was vividly described by Jesus in answer to the question that His disciples asked Him about the destruction of the Holy City (Mark 13:1). Jesus said to them, "There shall not be one stone upon another, that shall not be thrown down" (Mark 13:2). In what has been called "the Olivet Discourse" (because it was told on the Mount of Olives), Jesus described the tribulation of "those days" as the abomination of desolation spoken of by the prophet Daniel (Mark 13:14). This is referenced in Matthew 24:1-22, Mark 13:14-30, and Luke 21:5-24. In each of these Gospels, the same description is given by Jesus wherewith He warns the Jews to stay away from Jerusalem, saying "And when ye shall see Jerusalem compassed with armies, then know that the desolation thereof is near. Then let them which are in Judaea flee to the mountains; and let them which are in the midst of it depart out; and let not them that are in the countries enter thereinto. For these be the days of vengeance, that all things which are written may be fulfilled. But woe unto them that are with child, and to them that give suck in those days, for there shall be great distress in the land, and wrath upon this people! And they shall fall by the edge of the sword, and shall be led away captive into all nations: and Jerusalem shall be trodden down of the Gentiles, until the times of the Gentiles be fulfilled" (Luke 21:20-24).

What Jesus was warning about was the siege of Jerusalem that would take place in 70 A.D. However, as foretold by the LORD, there was a foreshadowing before that siege began. Four years earlier, in 66 A.D., the Roman General Cestius Gallus laid siege to the Holy City; but for inexplicable reasons, he abandoned the campaign after just nine days. Though his retreat to the coast may have been inexplicable in logical terms, it made perfect sense in spiritual terms: the LORD had answered the prayers of those who were caught in this first siege. The followers of Jesus glorified God for this and subsequently recognized it as the warning He had given them about the destruction that would befall Jerusalem "in their generation." However, those who were less familiar with the LORD's teaching, such as non-Christians and lukewarm believers, did not take heed of His warning. Consequently, they got caught in the second siege, which took place four years later under the Roman general Titus. It was the siege that Jesus called "an affliction such as was not from the beginning of the creation which God created unto this time, neither shall be" (Mark 13:19).

During the siege, the rampant starvation and accumulated waste amounted to a very slow and agonizing death both emotionally and physically for the Jews who were caught in the Holy City. Out of desperation, they began to pillage, murder, and cannibalize one another. In one detailed account, an eminent woman, under pain of starvation, had killed her infant son and roasted him. Then, after having eaten half his body, concealed the other half. When some desperate seditious Jews smelled the scent of the dead body, they threatened to end the life of the mother unless she showed them where the food was hidden. She replied that she had saved the best part for them. Then, uncovering the remains of the little boy, she said, "Come, eat of this food; for I have eaten of it myself. Do not you pretend to be more tender than a woman, or more compassionate than a mother." At this, even those seditious men were horrified, and word of what was done spread throughout the starving city.

According to another account, the Romans, after plundering the city, crucified many of the Jews, approximately five hundred per day. The soldiers amused themselves by nailing their victims in different postures and positions. The total number slain, including women and children, was estimated to be thirty-six hundred on a single occasion. All told, some three million Jews were

Model of the Second Temple, Jerusalem, Israel
Mikhail Semenov / Shutterstock.com

entrapped in the city. So numerous were the killings and atrocities that "the ground did not appear visible because of the number of bodies that lay upon it." In summary, the historian Flavius Josephus wrote: "the multitude of those that perished therein exceeded all the destructions that either men or God ever brought upon the world."

Beyond the agonizing starvation and violence, the siege was spiritually torturous. Upon their return to Rome, General Titus and his soldiers celebrated victory by parading the Menorah and Table of the Bread of God's Presence through the streets of the pagan city. Prior to this, these items had only been seen by the high priest of the Temple. Thus, the few Jews who survived the siege saw God mocked while at the same time feeling as though He had abandoned them after they had traveled, many of them long distances, to celebrate Passover in the Holy City. Under these circumstances, the temptation to renounce God would have been fierce.

The physical destruction of the Holy City was equally complete. Though conquering armies would normally convert an enemy fortress into their own stronghold, the Roman army deviated from this custom in the siege of Jerusalem because of their fierce disdain for the Jews. The Roman legions, which were also seeking revenge for their perceived defeat by Jewish Zealots in 66 A.D., did not leave one stone upon another, as foretold by Jesus.

In thinking about the tribulation of "those days," let us remember that Jesus was addressing His prophesy to the Jewish people, and for them, the destruction of the temple, the mockery made of the Holy place, and the unspeakable atrocities that occurred were the worst that the Jewish people, both individually and as a nation, had ever seen or ever would see. It was their "great tribulation." It was the complete embodiment of all that God had warned them about, not only through Jesus, but also through Moses (Lev. 26:14-45; Deut. 28:15-68).

Again Josephus, who had personally witnessed the siege and who no doubt was familiar with numerous destructive events prior to A.D. 70, including the great flood and other disasters recounted in the Old testament, is quoted as saying "the misfortunes of all men, from the beginning of the world, if they be compared to those of the Jews during the destruction of Jerusalem, are not so considerable as they are."

The additional detail given in Matt. 24:16-17 again makes it clear that this could not be the tribulation of the "last days" because those who were in Judea were warned by Jesus not to turn back but to flee to the mountains. Had this been referring to the tribulation of the last days there would be nowhere to hide because that tribulation leads directly to the end of the world. Of that tribulation we are also told that "the rest of those who were not killed by the plagues did not repent of their evil works" (Rev. 13:15). Thus, no one who will be caught in the tribulation of the last days will be saved either physically or spiritually. This is in contrast to the tribulation of "those days," which we are told would be shortened and that some would be saved (Matt. 24:15-22). Indeed, some Jews managed to survive the great tribulation only to be taken captive and sold on the slave market. Others were saved by taking heed of the LORD's warning and staying away from Jerusalem after the earlier siege in 66 A.D.

This should serve as a stern warning to us about the importance of prayerfully and thoughtfully studying the Bible. Indeed, the Holy Bible contains many other repeated warnings from Jesus, chief among them being the need to repent, the rapture of the church, and the tribulation of the last days, the latter which will occur after the "tribulation of those days" (the great tribulation) but not before the rapture (Matthew 24:36-51; Mark 13:23-27; 32-37; Luke 21:24-36). Also note that in referring to the great tribulation, Jesus said, "this generation shall not pass away till all these things be accomplished" (Matt. 24:34). This gives us a specific reference to the timing of the great tribulation: it would have to have occurred during the lifetime of at least some of those who were on earth during the time of Jesus. Jesus spoke the

Concept of the Lamb of God: The Lamb in front of the Cross of God

Paul Shuang / Shutterstock.com

prophesy in 33 A.D., and the siege of Jerusalem took place in 70 A.D. (just thirty-seven years later), thus fulfilling the prophesy.

REVELATION 6:12-14

And when he opened the sixth seal, I looked and saw that there was a great earthquake. And the sun became black as sackcloth of hair, and the moon became as blood. [13] And the stars of the sky fell to the earth, like a fig tree dropping its unripe figs when they are shaken by a great wind. [14] And the sky was removed like a scroll when it is rolled separately. And every mountain and island was moved out of its place.

Now comes the opening of the sixth seal and the beginning of the tribulation of the last days. Although Saint John describes this cataclysmic event the same way that Saint Mark does in Mark 13:24-25, one is literal, and the other is figurative. In Saint Mark's gospel, figurative language is used to announce the coming of the LORD with all His angels (Mark 13:26-27). The same language is used by Saint Matthew (Matt. 24:29). Note that in these two Gospels, the events portrayed will occur between "the tribulation of those days" (meaning the great tribulation) and the promised return of Jesus Christ. But in Rev. 6:12, the description is literal because we are at the end of the tribulation of the last days. Saint John writes, "The stars of heaven fell to the earth...and the heavens departed as a scroll when it is rolled together, and every island and mountain were moved out of their places" (Rev. 6:13-14). Saint Peter confirms that this is not merely figurative language. In 2 Peter 3:10, the apostle describes the same event in vivid detail, "...the heavens shall pass away with a great noise, and the elements will melt with fervent heat, and the earth also and the works that are in it shall be burned up." One would not use such physically precise detail if the description were strictly metaphorical. Literally speaking, the stars falling from heaven are likely meteorites and other celestial debris pelting the earth. Sometimes described as a "shooting star," a meteor is the trail of light that appears in the sky when a celestial body passes through the earth's atmosphere. The same destruction was described by Moses in Deuteronomy 32:22, in which Moses, speaking from God, foretold that the LORD would "consume the earth with her increase, and set on fire the foundations of the mountains."

REVELATION 6:15-17

And the kings of the earth, the princes, the commanders, the rich, the strong, and every slave and freeman hid themselves in the caves and in the rocks of the mountains. [16] And they told the mountains and the rocks, Fall on us, and hide us from the face of him who sits on the throne, and from the wrath of the Lamb; [17] for the great day of his wrath has come, and who is able to stand?

Note here that those who remained on the earth at that time hid from God and said to the mountains and rocks "fall on us." Like the cataclysmic events previously referenced, this statement could be interpreted either figuratively or literally. If it pertains to the siege of Jerusalem, it could be interpreted figuratively to mean "allow us to die." Whereas, if it pertains to the tribulation of the last days, it could be interpreted literally to mean that some of the inhabitants of the earth would actually hope that they would be killed by falling rocks, crumbling buildings, and other debris. The same wording is used in Luke 23:30, suggesting that Jesus was speaking figuratively about the siege of Jerusalem but also literally about the tribulation of the last days. Some of those who remain on earth

*Saint John the Evangelist by Charles Eyckens 1682
in Saint John the Baptist church, Brussels, Belgium*

Renata Sedmakova / Shutterstock.com

REVELATION CHAPTER 7 – THE SECOND VISION

after the rapture of the church will want to die both because they will realize that they have no means of escape and because they lack the hope that comes with true faith and repentance. For this reason, Saint John tells us that none of the inhabitants of the earth at that time will welcome the day of the LORD, and none will repent of their evil works. Instead, they will hide from God like Adam and Eve did after they had sinned in the garden of Eden. This is the first of many indicators in Revelation that the rapture of the church will occur *before* rather than during or after the start of the tribulation of the last days.

The Second Prophetic Vision

REVELATION 7:1-8

After this I saw four angels standing at the four corners of the earth, holding the four winds of the earth, so that no wind would blow on the earth, or on the sea, or on any tree. [2] And I saw another angel ascend from the east, having the seal of the living God; and he cried with a loud voice to the four angels to whom it was given to harm the earth and the sea, saying, [3] Do not harm the earth, neither the sea, nor the trees, until we have sealed the servants of our God on their foreheads. [4] And I beheld the number of those who were sealed: one hundred forty-four thousand out of every tribe of the children of Israel; [5] and of the tribe of Judah were sealed twelve thousand; of the tribe of Reuben, twelve thousand; of the tribe of Gad, twelve thousand; [6] of the tribe of Asher, twelve thousand; of the tribe of Naphtali, twelve thousand; of the tribe of Manasseh, twelve thousand; [7] of the tribe of Simeon, twelve thousand; of the tribe of Levi, twelve thousand; of the tribe of Issachar, twelve thousand; [8] of the tribe of Zebulun, twelve thousand; of the tribe of Joseph, twelve thousand; of the tribe of Benjamin were sealed twelve thousand.

The first words of this chapter, "And after these things..." are not intended to indicate a chronological continuation of what was said in Rev. 6. Rather, they are an introduction to Saint John's second vision.

In this vision, we are told the same prophesy again but with somewhat different images and symbolism. Here we are given an image of four angels standing on the four corners of the earth waiting for the pronouncement of the Day of the LORD. Here, the angels are told to hold back on executing God's judgment, which is in accord with Matthew 13:29, in which Jesus tells the parable of the servants allowing the wheat and the tares to grow together until the harvest. The rapture of the church is the beginning of the harvest; hence, God's judgment cannot begin until the faithful are "sealed in their foreheads." That is to say, until they are given time to grow spiritually in thought, reason, will, emotion, and language under the direction of the Holy Spirit. As explained earlier, the neural correlates of all of these cognitive-emotional functions are carried out by the frontal lobe of the brain, which is located just inside the forehead. Consistent with this vision, the Sacrament of Holy Unction (the application of a tincture of Holy oil to the forehead) has for centuries been used as a sign of being consecrated to God. In verses 4-8, we are told that those who are sealed are one hundred and forty-four thousand in number, which is symbolic of the faithful among the twelve tribes of Isreal. Note in

Fresco of four big Teachers of west catholic church by Agostino Pegrassi from year 1932 in San Bernardino church and Canossa chapel, Verona, Italy

Renata Sedmakova / Shutterstock.com

verse 11 that there are elders standing around the throne of God. Again we see that these servants are in God's kingdom before the rapture of the church. They are part of the "first resurrection" spoken of in Rev. 20. According to the Revelator, they have been reigning with Christ since the day of His resurrection. We are told in Matt.19:28 and Luke 22:30 that these faithful followers would sit on thrones to judge the twelve tribes of Israel. They will indeed do this when the unsaved Jews (and the rest of the unsaved) are called to judgment at the end of the world. Until then, those in the first resurrection will continue to reign with Christ (Rev. 3:21; 20:6).

REVELATION 7:9-14

After these things I looked, and behold, a great multitude, which no man could number, out of every nation, tribe, people, and tongue, standing before the throne and before the Lamb, dressed in white robes, with palm branches in their hands. [10] They cried with a loud voice, saying, Salvation be to our God, who sits on the throne, and to the Lamb! [11] And all the angels stood round about the throne, and the elders, and the four living creatures; and they fell on their faces before his throne and worshiped God, [12] saying, Amen! Blessing, glory, wisdom, thanksgiving, honor, power, and might be to our God forever and ever. Amen. [13] And one of the elders answered, saying to me, These you see arrayed in white robes, who are they, and from where did they come? [14] And I said to him, My lord, you know. And he said to me, These are those who came out of the great tribulation; they have washed their robes and made them white in the blood of the Lamb.

Verse 9 denotes the rapture of the church, which will include people from all walks of life. Here again we see that the elders, who are around the altar, are distinguished from the rest of the redeemed, who are gathered before the altar (vs. 11 and 13). In verse 13, the distinction between the elders and the rest of the saved is made clear by the question that one of the elders asks Saint John about those who are arrayed in white robes. In verse 14, the elder tells John that those in white robes were delivered from the great tribulation of the last days.

REVELATION 7:15-17

Therefore they are before the throne of God; they serve him day and night in his temple. And he who sits on the throne will shelter them. [16] They will never be hungry, neither thirsty any more; neither will the sun beat on them, nor any heat; [17] for the Lamb who is in the midst of the throne shepherds them, and leads them to fountains of living water. And God will wipe away every tear from their eyes.

Both the elders and the rest of the saved souls serve the LORD day and night; that is, continuously (vs. 15) just as they had done on earth. Likewise, the LORD will dwell among them and watch over them just as He did while they were on earth.

REVELATION 8:1-13

When he opened the seventh seal, there was silence in heaven for the space of about half an hour. [2] Then I saw the seven angels who stand before God, and seven trumpets were given to them. [3] Another angel came and stood before the altar; and a golden censer was given to him, and with it much incense, that he

The first plague of Egypt: water changed into blood. James Tissot

Courtesy of Wikipedia

might offer it with the prayers of all the saints upon the golden altar which was before the throne. [4] And the smoke of the incense, with the prayers of all the saints went up before God out of the angel's hand. [5] And the angel took the censer and filled it with the fire from the altar, and threw it onto the earth. And there followed thunders, and sounds, and lightnings, and an earthquake. [6] And the seven angels who had the seven trumpets prepared themselves to sound. [7] The first sounded, and there followed hail and fire mixed with water, and they were poured out upon the earth. And one-third of the earth was burned up, and one-third of the trees were burned up, and all green grass was burned up. [8] Then the second angel sounded, and something like a great mountain burning with fire was thrown into the sea; one-third of the sea became blood, [9] one-third of the living creatures which were in the sea died, and one-third of the ships were destroyed. [10] The third angel sounded, and a great star fell from the sky, burning like a torch, and fell upon one-third of the rivers, and upon the springs of the waters. [11] The name of the star is called Wormwood. And one-third of the waters became wormwood. Many people died from the waters because they were made bitter. [12] The fourth angel sounded, and one-third of the sun was struck, and one-third of the moon, and one-third of the stars; so that one-third of them was darkened, and the day would not shine for one-third of it, and the night likewise. [13] And I saw and heard an eagle, with a tail red as it were blood, flying through the midst of heaven, saying with a loud voice, Woe! Woe! Woe! to those who dwell on the earth, for coming are the sounds of the trumpets of the three angels, which are yet to sound!

Now, with the church harvested and taken out of harm's way, the wrath of God is ready to be unleashed upon all those who are left behind. In verse 2 this is depicted as seven angels with trumpets and an angel with a censor. With fire the angel casts the censor down to the earth (vs. 5), "and there were voices, and thunderings, and lightnings, and an earthquake." Note that this is the same way that the tribulation of the last days is described in Saint John's first prophetic vision (Rev. 6:12). There we read: "...and, lo, there was a great earthquake; and the sun became black as sackcloth of hair, and the moon became as blood..." Then, with the sounding of the trumpets (Rev. 8:8-12), the inhabitants of the earth are inflicted with plagues, some of them like the plagues that were wrought through Moses in Egypt (Exod. 7-12).

The sounding of the first angel (vs. 7) appears to be a description of war on earth and its consequences. That there would be war during the tribulation of the last days was also prophesied by Zechariah, who wrote: "And it shall come to pass in that day, that a great tumult from the LORD shall be among them; and they shall lay hold every one on the hand of his neighbor, and his hand shall rise up against the hand of his neighbor" (Zech. 14:13).

With the sounding of the second angel we are told that "a great mountain burning with fire was cast into the sea." This would seem to be a large volcanic eruption causing lava to be poured out into the ocean, affecting ships and making local waters uninhabitable to marine life.

With the sounding of the third angel (verses 10 and 11) we are told that "a great star fell from heaven, burning as it were a lamp, and fell into the water." We could assume this to be a large

Oil pumps on fire background
Krasowit / Shutterstock.com

meteorite, a supposition that would be consistent with the previous reference to "stars falling from the sky" (Matt. 24:29). Meteorites are often referred to as "falling stars" because of the trail of light that they leave behind. The description of "a third part of the waters becoming wormwood" means that they were made bitter; that is, undrinkable.

REVELATION 9:1-19

The fifth angel sounded, and I saw a star fall from heaven to the earth. And to him was given the key to the bottomless pit. [2] He opened the pit, and smoke went up out of the abyss, like the smoke from a burning furnace. And the sun and the air were darkened because of the smoke that ascended from the abyss. [3] And out of the smoke came locusts upon the earth; and power was given to them, as the scorpions of the earth have power. [4] And they were told that they should not harm the grass of the earth, neither any green thing, neither any tree, but only those men who did not have the seal of God on their foreheads. [5] And they were ordered not to kill but to torment them for five months. Their torment was like the torment of a scorpion when it strikes a person. [6] In those days men will seek death, and will not find it; they will desire to die, and death will flee from them. [7] The shapes of the locusts were like horses prepared for war. On their heads were something like crowns of gold, and their faces were like the faces of men. [8] They had hair like women's hair, and their teeth were like the teeth of lions. [9] They had breastplates, as though they were breastplates of iron; and the sound of their wings was like the sound of the chariots of many horses rushing into battle. [10] They had tails like those of scorpions, and there were stings in their tails. And they had power to hurt men for five months. [11] They had over them as king the angel of the bottomless pit. His name in Hebrew is Abaddon, but in Greek it is Apollyon. [12] The first woe is past. Behold, there are still two more woes to come. [13] The sixth angel sounded, and I heard a voice from the horns of the golden altar which is before God, [14] saying to the sixth angel who had the trumpet, Free the four angels who are bound by the great river Euphrates. [15] And the four angels were freed, those who had been prepared for that hour and day and month and year, so that they might kill one-third of mankind. [16] The number of the armies of the horsemen was two-hundred million. I heard the number of them. [17] Thus I saw the horses in the vision, and those who sat on them, having breastplates of fiery red, hyacinth blue, and sulfur yellow; and the horses' heads resembled lions' heads. Out of their mouths proceeded fire, smoke, and sulfur. [18] By these three plagues were one-third of mankind killed: by the fire, the smoke, and the sulfur, which issued out of their mouths. [19] For the power of the horses is in their mouths and in their tails. For their tails were like serpents and had heads, and with them they did harm.

St. Michael Vanquishing Satan (1518) by Raphael, depicting Satan being cast out of heaven by Michael the Archangel

Courtesy of Wikipedia

Here the description momentarily turns symbolic, as the next star that falls from heaven is a king who is referred to as the "angel of the bottomless pit" (vs. 11). We are told that when this king opened the seal of the pit, thick smoke billowed out to the extent that darkness fell upon the whole region during broad daylight. Coming out of the smoke came ground troops dressed in battle garb. These troops were apparently ordered not to kill anyone (vs. 5-6) but rather to let them suffer as much as possible just as general Titus allowed the Jews to suffer as much as possible during the siege of Jerusalem. The name of the king in Hebrew is Abaddon and in Greek Apollyon, which is translated "king of destruction." Who this king is we are not old, but it is possible that he will set fire to oil wells that fuel the war machine of his enemies just as the president of Iraq did when the U.S. invaded Kuwait during Dessert Storm. According to eyewitness reports at the time, the smoke from the burning oil wells was so thick that there was continual darkness over the region until the wells were finally capped. The fall of the king in Saint John's vision is referred to as a "falling star." The same imagery is used in the book of Isaiah when the prophet makes reference to the fall of King Nebuchadnezzar (Isa. 14:12).

Revelation vs. 3-19 clearly tell us that there will be a great battle amidst the various other plagues that will befall the earth during the tribulation of the last days. This is to be expected, for if we can hardly maintain peace on earth when the Spirit of God dwells among us, how could there possibly be peace after He has left the world with the children of God?

Revelation 9:21

The rest of mankind, who were not killed by these plagues, did not repent of the works of their hands, that they should stop worshipping demons, and the idols of gold, and of silver, and of brass, and of stone, and of wood; which cannot see nor hear. [21] They did not repent of their murders, their sorceries, their sexual immorality, or their thefts.

Here again we are told that those who are not killed by the various plagues of the tribulation of the last days will not repent of their evil deeds. Hence, there could be no followers of Christ left on earth. This repeated reference, and the consistent chronology of the first two visions, provide indisputable evidence that the rapture of the church will precede the tribulation of the last days.

Revelation 10:1-4

And I saw a mighty angel coming down from heaven, clothed with a cloud. And the rainbow of the cloud was upon his head. His face was like the sun, and his feet, like pillars of fire. [2] And he had in his hand a little open book. And he set his right foot on the sea, and his left on the land; [3] and he cried with a loud voice, as a lion roars. When he cried, the seven thunders uttered their voices. [4] And when the seven thunders had spoken, I was about to write; but I heard a voice from heaven saying, Seal up the things which the seven thunders have uttered, and do not write them.

These verses are an introduction to Saint John's third prophetic vision. The word "angel" means messenger of God. That the angel was clothed with a cloud and had a rainbow upon his head means symbolically that he was gloriously arrayed. That his face shown like the sun and his feet were like pillars of fire means that he was the bearer of light and truth. That one foot was on the earth and the the other on the sea means that the angel had complete dominion.

Painting of Vision of St. John the Evangelist on the Patmos (Apocalypse) island in Basilica de San Vicente church by unknown artist of 17th century

Renata Sedmakova / Shutterstock.com

REVELATION 10:5-7

And the angel who I saw standing on the sea and on the land lifted up his right hand to heaven, [6] and swore by him who lives forever and ever, who created heaven and the things that are in it, the earth and the things that are in it, and the sea and the things that are in it, that there should be no more delay of time, [7] but in the days of the voice of the seventh angel, when he shall begin to sound, the mystery of God shall be fulfilled, as he declared to his servants, the prophets.

That which the angel was not to write was the mystery of God. The mystery of God cannot be written because God is infinite, and as such He cannot be defined through writing, speech, or in any human way. As amazing as man's capabilities are, they are but dust in comparison to those of Almighty God. Likewise, the vast expanse of God's creation—the moon, the stars, and the far reaches of space—as majestic and unfathomable as they are, are just a shadow, a crude prototype of the world to come. As Saint Paul wrote, "Eye hath not seen, nor ear heard, neither have entered into the heart of man, the things which God has prepared for those who love him" (1 Cor. 2:9). Indeed, the things that God is preparing for His faithful servants are unimaginable. And they will be coming soon because life on earth is, for any individual, very short. That there would "no longer be delay" means that the mystery of God was, likewise, to be revealed very soon in the light of eternity. When the seventh angel begins to sound, the New World order will be established, and the kingdoms of this world will become the kingdom of God (Rev. 11:15).

The Third Prophetic Vision

REVELATION 10:8-11

And the same voice I heard from heaven spoke to me again, saying, Go, take the little book which is open in the hand of the angel who stands on the sea and on the land. [9] And I went to the angel, and as I was about to ask him for the little book, he said to me, Take it, and eat it; and it will make your stomach bitter, but in your mouth it will be as sweet as honey. [10] So I took the little book out of the hand of the angel, and ate it up. In my mouth it was sweet as honey, but it made my stomach bitter. [11] Then he said to me, You must prophesy again about many peoples, nations, languages, and kings.

Here begins the third prophetic vision, which Saint John introduces with the statement: "And the voice I heard from heaven spoke to me again." With this, the prophet tells us that he was told to "take the little book and eat it," which is a Near-eastern expression that means he is being given another revelation of truth. To prepare him for this vision, Saint John is warned that what he is about to see would make his "stomach bitter" but taste as "sweet as honey." These are Near-eastern expressions that mean that the truth that is about to be revealed will be hard to stomach, or "hard to swallow"; yet because it is the truth, it will be sweet in comparison to the bitterness of lies.

Moses with the Tablets of the Law, 1624, by Guido Reni
Courtesy of Wikipedia

REVELATION 11:1-2

And a reed like a rod was given to me, and the angel stood and said, Arise and measure the temple of God, and the altar, and those who worship in it. [2] But leave out the court which is outside of the temple, and do not measure it, for it has been given to the gentiles. They will tread the holy city under foot for forty-two months.

Saint John is told to measure God's Temple, the altar, and the worshipers. The word "measure" as we understand it today does not seem appropriate here because there is no reference to anything being built, nor would it make sense to take measurements of the worshipers. According to the late Near-eastern Bible scholar Dr. George M. Lamsa, and in gratitude for the continued work of Dr. Rocco Errico, who studied extensively under Dr. Lamsa, the Aramaic word *Meshakh* has two meanings: to "measure" and to "anoint." With only thirteen letters to the alphabet, there were many words in the ancient Aramaic language that had more than one meaning. With this in mind, it is clear that the word "anoint" is the more appropriate meaning here. The "reed like a rod" (vs. 1) refers to a staff that Bishops of the church sometimes hold at their side and rest their arm upon. Here, the angel instructs Saint John to anoint the temple and the worshipers but to omit the outer court. The outer court, we are told, is given to the gentiles. This was to symbolize what was soon to occur; namely, that the Holy City would be surrounded by the Roman army (the gentiles). This prophesy was fulfilled in 70 A.D. when Roman garrisons besieged Jerusalem under general Titus (vs.2). It should come as no surprise that Saint John sees so many visions of the siege of Jerusalem. First, it was soon to take place; and second, it would be the greatest disaster ever to befall the Jewish people both individually and as a nation.

REVELATION 11:3-4

I will give power to my two witnesses, and they will prophesy one thousand two hundred and sixty days, clothed in sackcloth. [4] These are the two olive trees and the two candlesticks, standing before the LORD of the earth.

The "two witnesses" is a reference to the fact that the Mosaic law required the testimony of two persons to be binding. Also, that the two witnesses referred to by Saint John had the power to hold back the rain, turn the waters into blood, and smite the earth with plagues suggests that, more specifically, he was also referring to Moses and Elijah. In Exodus 7:20 we are told that Moses, in the sight of Pharaoh and his servants, lifted up the rod and struck the waters that were in the river, "and all the waters that were in the river were turned to blood." This was one of the many plagues that Moses prophesied to the nobility of Egypt. In the eighteenth chapter of the first book of Kings, we are told that Elijah called rain down from heaven in the sight of Ahab during the famine that fell upon Samaria. Moses and Elijah are also described as two olive trees, which means bearers of peace, and two candlesticks, which means bearers of light. The prophets were the bearers of God's light, which promotes peace and reconciliation between contentious parties. Moses and Elijah were also two witnesses in that they supernaturally conversed with Jesus on the mount of transfiguration (Matt. 17:1-3; Mark 9:2-4; Luke 9:28-32).

In a broader sense, the two witnesses can be thought of as the teachings of the Old and New Testaments of the Holy Bible (the prophets and the apostles). These teachings will hold the unbelievers accountable on the day of judgment. That the two witnesses are "clothed in sackcloth" (vs. 3) means that the words of the old and new testaments were conveyed with true love and humility. Sackcloth was an uncomfortable material that in the biblical days was worn for a time as a

Saint Elijah, altarpiece on the main altar of Saint Eliah church in Lipnik, Croatia
Ruskpp / Shutterstock.com

show of repentance. In the book of Ester, we are told that when Mordecai learned of the king's decree against his brethren, "he put on sackcloth with ashes and cried in the streets with a loud, bitter cry" (Est. 4:1). The prophets and apostles prayed and fasted as they sought God's help for their brethren, and they mourned for those who rejected the word of God.

REVELATION 11:5

If anyone desires to harm them, fire will proceed out of their mouths and devour their enemies. If anyone desires to harm them, he must be killed in the same manor.

The fire that proceeds out of the mouths of the two witnesses is the word of God. In Rev. 19:15, we are told that a two-edged sword proceeded out of the mouth of Jesus to smite the nations. The "two-edged sword" is the Word of God, which separates right from wrong, good from bad, and truth from error. Jesus was speaking through the two witnesses.

REVELATION 11:6

These have the power to shut up the sky, that it may not rain during the days of their prophecy. And they have power over the waters, to turn them into blood, and to strike the earth with every plague, as often as they will.

This verse points back to the judgments that God wrought through the two witnesses while they were on earth.

REVELATION 11:7

When they have finished their testimony, the beast that comes up from the bottomless pit will make war against them, and overcome them, and kill them.

Here we are told that God's faithful servants are protected until their work on earth is completed. After that, God is faithful to provide them a death both for His glory and for the salvation of souls. Throughout history, God's faithful servants have been mocked, imprisoned, tortured, and killed for preaching the Gospel of Jesus Christ (vs. 7). However, we are also told that those who put them to death will in like manner be killed (vs. 5). In his letter to the Galatians, Saint Paul reminds us that " you will reap what you sow" (Gal. 6:7). What's more, the testimony that the opponents of Christ attempt to suppress will hold them accountable on the day of judgment.

The beast that ascends out of the bottomless pit and makes war against the two witnesses refers to the evil in the world that would overpower God's servants physically but not spiritually. This would temporarily give the evil doers a sense of victory, which they would flaunt by mocking the teachings of Christ. For a time, they will appear to prevail. Their apparent victory is symbolized by "the dead bodies of the prophets laying in the streets." That those who dwell on the earth make merry over them and care not to put them in graves symbolizes the cold-heartedness and pride of the unbelievers. It also refers to the weak commitment of those who are religiously-minded but spiritually dead. During the siege of Jerusalem, many such persons had traveled to the Holy City in observance of Passover and undoubtedly felt betrayed by God when they unexpectedly found themselves hemmed in by the Romans. That such persons would let the dead bodies of the prophets "lie in the streets" means that they became angry at God during the time of testing and departed from the faith. Not surprisingly, many of these Jews also retaliated against each other during the siege, as the number of Jews who were killed by one another during the siege was far greater than those who were killed by the Roman soldiers. In a broader sense, the disrespecting of the dead bodies symbolizes the retaliation against God by all persons who ignore, deny, and distort the truth (vs. 9-10).

Le Sainte Bible: Traduction nouvelle selon la Vulgate par Mm. J.-J. Bourasse et P. Janvier Tours: Alfred Mame et Fils. 2) 1866 3) France 4) Gustave Doré

Ruskpp / Shutterstock.com

The disregard for God's word by unbelievers would not go on for very long (vs. 11). Eschatologically, the short period of time that the dead bodies of the prophets would lie in the streets tells us that the length of time between the period of unbelief by "people and kindreds and tongues and nations" and the rapture of the church would be very short. This is further supported by 1:Tim. 4:1-3 and Matt. 24:12, in which we are told that in the latter times some will depart from the faith and "the love of many will wax cold."

REVELATION 11:8

And their dead bodies will lie in the street of the great city, which spiritually is called Sodom and Egypt, where also their LORD was crucified.

That their bodies "lay dead in the street" is again symbolic of the deaf ear that the corrupt have for the word of God. Saint John's reference to "the great city where our LORD was crucified" as spiritual Sodom and Egypt is to say that Jerusalem was as corrupt as Sodom, Gomorrah, and Egypt. Clearly that was true, for it was the place where Jesus was betrayed, arrested, and put to death. The crucifixion of Jesus was the greatest atrocity and injustice ever committed by humankind. Those who perpetrated this act had turned a deaf ear to the words of the prophets and the love of God.

REVELATION 11:9-10

And their dead bodies will be looked upon by peoples, and tribes, and nations, and tongues for three and a half days, but they will not allow the bodies to be laid in graves. [10] And those who dwell on the earth will rejoice over them, and make merry; and they will give gifts to one another, because these two prophets tormented those who dwell on the earth.

That the dead bodies of the two witnesses were ignored by "people and kindreds and tongues and nations" symbolizes the widespread disregard that humanity has for the LORD. That they did not even put their bodies into graves but rather rejoiced over their demise is symbolic of the fact that most of humanity has no respect for biblical teaching and would prefer that it be done away with.

REVELATION 11:11

And after the three and a half days, the spirit of life from God entered into them, and they stood on their feet; and a great fear fell on those who saw them.

That they came to life after three and a half days refers to the fact that Moses and Elijah have already been resurrected. They were part of the first resurrection referred to in Rev. 20:5-6. All of God's most faithful servants have already been or will be resurrected immediately after they die just as Jesus was. Although the three and a half days represents an indeterminate period of time, the brevity of it symbolizes what little power death has over God's faithful servants. Like Jesus, they cannot be held in the grave for very long (Acts 2:24-24). The three and a half days also refers to the brevity of time before the promised return of Jesus Christ.

REVELATION 11:12

And I heard a loud voice from heaven saying to them, Come up here! And they ascended to heaven in a cloud, and their enemies watched them.

The return of Jesus Christ and the general resurrection is referred to symbolically in this verse. That the two witnesses ascended to heaven as the others watched them is a reference to the rapture of the church. Their ascent to heaven "in a cloud" is a reference to the way Jesus was taken up to heaven as He spoke to His disciples on the

Victor Vasnetsov's The Last Judgment, 1904

Courtesy of Wikipedia

Mount of Olives (Acts 1:9-12). All those who are in Christ will ascend to heaven in the same way that Jesus did.

Revelation 11:13

In the same hour there was a great earthquake, and a tenth part of the city fell. Seven thousand people were killed in the earthquake, and those who remained were terrified, and gave glory to the God.

Here again we see the consistency in the chronology of events portrayed in each of Saint John's visions. After the rapture of the church, which is symbolized by the ascent of the two witnesses, the tribulation of the last days begins. As in the first prophetic vision described in Rev. 6:12 - 8:4, and the second prophetic vision described in Rev. 8:5 - 10:7, the tribulation of the last days begins with a great earthquake. That those who were left behind gave glory to God in heaven (vs. 13) means that they acknowledged God's sovereign authority over them, but that they were afraid means that they knew that their end was near. Those who are followers of Jesus will rejoice at His coming, whereas those who are against Him will despair at His coming (Heb. 10:26-27).

Revelation 11:14-15

The second woe is past. Behold, the third woe comes quickly. [15] The seventh angel sounded, and there were great voices in heaven, saying, The kingdoms of this world have become the kingdom of our Lord, and of his Christ; and he shall reign forever and ever.

As in the second prophetic vision, the sounding of the seventh angel signifies the end of the tribulation of the last days and the consummation of the New Heaven and the New Earth, when the kingdoms of this world become the kingdoms of our God and of His Christ.

Revelation 11:16-17

And the twenty-four elders, who sat before God on their seats, fell on their faces and worshiped God, [17] saying, We give you thanks, O Lord God the Almighty, who is and who was, because thou have taken to thyself thy great power, and reigned.

The elders give glory to God for remaining true to His word and establishing the New World order.

Revelation 11:18

And the nations were angry, for your wrath came, and the time of the dead, that they should be judged, and to reward your servants, the prophets and saints and all those who fear your name, small and great; and to destroy those who destroy the earth.

With the establishment of God's eternal kingdom, it is time to summon the departed souls who, having not been part of either the first or second resurrection, would still be in their graves.

Revelation 11:19

And the temple of God in heaven was opened, and the ark of the Lord's covenant was seen in his temple. And there were lightnings, and thunders, and voices, and an earthquake, and a great hailstorm.

As seen elsewhere in the Bible, the "lightnings, and voices, and thunderings, and an earthquake, and great hail" announce the end of one grand event and the beginning of another. There was a great

Saint John the Evangelist on Patmos, 1490

Nancy Bauer / Shutterstock.com

earthquake immediately after Jesus, while hanging on the cross, uttered the words, "It is finished," (John 19:30; Matt. 27:50-51), and there was a great earthquake on the dawning of the first day, when Jesus was resurrected from the grave (Matt. 28:1-2). Likewise, in the book of Exodus, we are told that there were thunders and lightenings and that the whole mount quaked greatly when The LORD came down upon mount Sinai and spoke to Moses (Exod. 19:16-20). Note that these earthquakes were not coincident seismic eruptions but rather spiritual quakes that were caused by the power of the Holy Spirit.

The Fourth Prophetic Vision

REVELATION 12:1-3

And a great sign was seen in heaven: a woman clothed with the sun, and the moon under her feet, and on her head a crown of twelve stars. [2] And she being with child cried out in pain, laboring to give birth. [3] And another sign was seen in heaven. Behold, a great red dragon, having seven heads and ten horns, and on his heads, seven crowns.

Here begins the fourth prophetic vision with the woman "clothed with the sun," having a crown of twelve stars. This is a reference to the Blessed Virgin Mary, and the crown of twelve stars represents the twelve Apostles. Then, with the birth of Jesus Christ, we are introduced to His adversary, the "great red dragon having seven heads and ten horns and seven crowns upon his heads" (vs. 3). The great red dragon is symbolic of the opposition that Jesus Christ would face. Thus, this vision begins with a spiritual battle between good and evil—Christ verses the dragon. However, within the context of the political and religious climate in which Saint John received the vision, the dragon specifically represented the Roman Empire with its haughty pride and insatiable quest for power. The seven heads with crowns upon his heads could be the succession of the seven kings of Rome—Romulus, Pompilius, Hositilius, Marcius, Priscus, Tullius, and Superbus. Similarly, the ten horns could be the ten Roman Emperors that followed them—Julius Caesar, Augustus Caesar, Tiberius Caesar, Gaius Caesar (Caligula), Claudius Caesar, Nero Caesar, Vespasian Caesar, Titus Caesar, Domitian Caesar, and Trajan Caesar. The seven heads and ten horns of the dragon correspond to the twelve stars on Saint Mary's crown because the heads and horns of the dragon carried out his will just as the twelve disciples carried out the will of Jesus, who was the crown on Mary's head and the antithesis of the dragon.

Note here that events that clearly occurred on earth (the Immaculate Conception and the birth of Jesus) appear in Saint John's vision as a "great wonder in heaven." That tells us that events that the Apostle sees taking place in heaven actually refer to events on earth. In Rev. 15:1 he says, "And I saw another sign in heaven." The phrase "sign in heaven" is a metaphorical way of saying "vision from God." Such visions come from above, from God in heaven. Hence, the place where the sign appears is not necessarily the place where the event is taking place or will take place.

REVELATION 12:4

And his tail drew one third of the stars of heaven, and cast them down to the earth. And the dragon stood before the woman who was ready to give birth, so that he might devour her child as soon as the child was born.

Here we are told that the dragon *drew* a third part of the stars of heaven and cast them to the earth.

Fiery Furnace, 1266 by Toros Roslin

Courtesy of Wikipedia

These stars are not fallen angels but rather persons, tribes, and nations who were lifted up by God's grace but subsequently cast down by their pride and self-reliance.

In seeking to properly understand difficult passages of the Bible, we need to compare scripture with scripture. In other parts of the Bible, "stars" refer to people and, in some cases, entire nations. In Rev. 1, the "stars" are specifically defined as the elders of the seven churches, and in Rev. 12:1, the Blessed Virgin is pictured as a woman clothed with the sun wearing a crown of twelves stars (the twelve apostles). In the book of Isaiah, King Nebuchadnezzar is referred to as the "morning star" that goes down to the pit (Isa. 14:12;19), and in Rev. 22:16, the LORD Jesus Christ is referred to as "the bright and morning star." As previously stated, stars can also refer to nations and peoples, such as the Hebrews, the Babylonians, and the Romans. These nations were lifted up by God's grace but fell from their lofty positions as a consequence of their pride. The entire book of Ezekiel is addressed to the consequences of national pride and idolatry. As previously stated, the revelations that Saint John receives from above actually refer to events on earth (Rev. 12:1-2). Thus, "the third part of the stars of heaven" more aptly represents people, tribes, and nations. Also, the idea that the dragon (who metaphorically represents Satan) had cast a host of angels down to the earth does not square up with the idea that Satan and his angels waged war against God and His angels. Had such a war actually occurred, Satan would have been defeating himself by casting his own comrades down to the earth. Moreover, had there really been a war in heaven, the dragon would have been cast out as well. Hence, the "stars" that Saint John is referring to in Rev. 12:4 do not appear to be angelic beings but rather persons and peoples on earth of high notoriety, power, or status. The same metaphor is still being used today when we refer to famous people as "rock stars," "movie stars," and "football stars."

In the biblical days, the leaders of the early church were regarded as stars because they held authoritative positions, and the three boys, Shadrach, Meshach, and Abednego, who had been thrown into the fiery furnace, were regarded as stars after they miraculously emerged from the fiery flames completely unharmed (Dan. 1:18, 3:8-30, 4:20-25, 5:18-20, 8:10). In Isaiah 14, King Nebuchadnezzar is referred to as the "morning star" because he was such a feared and powerful leader, and Daniel was worshipped as a star after he interpreted the king's dream (Dan. 2:46).

That brings us back to the question: how is it that the dragon drew a third part of the stars of heaven and cast them down to the earth? The answer is that the dragon is symbolic of pride, and pride leads to errors in judgment that cause many persons and sometimes entire nations to fall from their positions of prominence. Pride caused King Nebuchadnezzar to "fall from heaven" (Isa. 14:4-12), and it caused King Herod to fall after he ordered the mass execution of innocent children in an effort to destroy baby Jesus. Similarly, the nation of Israel was said to have been "cast down from heaven" after she fell to the Babylonians in 586 B.C. (Lam 2:1), and the Roman Empire, which was the epitome of pride, lost her position of prominence when she fell to Germanic tribes during the fourth and fifth centuries. As it is written, "pride goeth before the fall" (Prv. 16:18).

Note the care with which Saint John chooses his words: pride does not force us; rather, it "draws" us. Verse 4 reads, "the dragon drew a third part of the stars of heaven and cast them down to the earth." Pride draws us down from high positions by the allure of thinking that the self is invincible. The two-thirds of the stars who the dragon was unable to cast down to the earth were faithful persons of notoriety, such as Daniel, Shadrach, Meshach, Abednego, John the Baptist, the prophets, the saints, and, of course, Jesus Christ Himself. These great stars of God did not allow their popularity and success to rob them of their humility. Instead, they continued to acknowledge their dependency upon

Paint of Virgin mary and the saint in church San Fermo Maggiore by M. G. Falconetto 1504, Verona, Italy

Renata Sedmakova / Shutterstock.com

God (Matt. 4:1-11). Thus, the image of a dragon drawing a third part of the stars of heaven down to the earth is a warning about the dangers of pride.

REVELATION 12:5

And she gave birth to a son, a male child, who was to rule all the nations with a rod of iron. And her child was caught up to God, and to his throne.

That Jesus would rule the nations with a "rod of iron" is symbolic of the surpassing power of the truth. In the first century, iron was the strongest material known to man. All other metals could be hammered with iron.

REVELATION 12:6

And the woman fled into the wilderness, where she has a place prepared by God, that she may be nourished there one thousand, two hundred and sixty days.

This is a reference to the Blessed Virgin Mary and Saint Joseph fleeing to Egypt to escape the evil dictate of King Herod (Matt. 2:13).

REVELATION 12:7

And there was war in heaven. Michael and his angels fought against the dragon; and the dragon and his angels fought.

This war in heaven, described as Michael and his angels fighting against the dragon and his angels, is a spiritual battle. It symbolically represents the battle that Jesus would wage against the pride of humanity, which again is symbolized by the dragon.

REVELATION 12:8

But the dragon and his angels did not prevail, neither was their place found anymore in heaven.

Michael and his angels represent the spirit of humility, which conquers pride. Humility conquers pride because it is based on truth, whereas pride is based on falsehood. The LORD's followers adhered to the truth and remained loyal to God to the end, thereby conquering the dragon and all those who think like him.

REVELATION 12:9

The great dragon was thrown down, that old serpent, who is called the devil and Satan, the deceiver of the whole world. He was thrown down to the earth, and his angels were thrown down with him.

That the great dragon was cast down to the earth is a reiteration of the fact that pride, which the dragon represents, goes before the fall. The angels who were cast out with him were those who thought like him.

REVELATION 12:10-11

And I heard a loud voice in heaven, saying, Now the salvation, the power, and the kingdom of our God, and the authority of his Christ have come; for the accuser of our brethren has been thrown down, who accused them before our God day and night. [11] They overcame him by the blood of the Lamb, and by the word of their testimony. And they did not spare their lives, even to death.

These verses refer to the teachings of Jesus Christ, His resurrection from the dead and the testimony of saints. The accuser of our brothers is the spirit of pride, which refuses to submit to God's sovereign authority. That pride was "thrown down" means that it was overcome by the spirit of humility. Again, these verses do not refer to a literal battle in the kingdom of God. The kingdom

Ruins of the great Colosseum, Rome, Italy
Studio Dagdagaz / Shutterstock.com

of God has always been and always will be a place of perfect peace, harmony, and love. The war in heaven described in Rev. 12:7 metaphorically represents the spiritual battle between truth and error. That this battle took place on earth becomes clear when we compare Rev. 12:7 with Rev. 12:11. Verse 12:7 tells us that the war in heaven was between two sets of angels, but verse 12:11 tells us that our brothers overcame them. "Our brothers" are not angels in heaven but rather our fellow believers on earth. Our fellow believers (the prophets and the saints) overcame the proud with the spirit of humility. Again, Saint John describes the events as happening in the heavens because that is where he sees the visions; but the events themselves are happening or will happen on earth.

REVELATION 12:12

Therefore rejoice, O heavens, and all you who dwell in them. And woe to the inhabitants of the earth and the sea! Because the devil has gone down to you; and his wrath is great, knowing that he has but a short time.

The devil coming down in great wrath refers to the anger of the proud when their self-deception is exposed by the truth and they fall from their place of vain glory. They know that their time is short because life on earth and all of its trappings are only temporary.

REVELATION 12:13-16

And when the dragon saw that he was thrown down to the earth, he pursued the woman who had given birth to a male child. [14] And two wings of a great eagle were given to the woman, that she might fly into the wilderness, out of the presence of the serpent, where she might be nourished for a time, and times, and half a time. [15] And the serpent spewed water out of his mouth like a river after the woman, that he might cause her to be carried away by the flood. [16] But the earth helped the woman; it opened its mouth and swallowed up the river which the dragon spewed out of his mouth.

When King Herod heard that a king had been born among the Jews, his pride was threatened because his false kingship was in jeopardy. In his wrath he sought to pursue Jesus and His mother by issuing a decree that all the children in Bethlehem be killed. But the angel of the LORD appeared to Joseph in a dream and warned him to flee with Mary and Jesus into the Egyptian desert (Matt. 2:116). A reference is also made to the way God delivered the Hebrew slaves out of the hands of Pharaoh when He parted the waters of the Red Sea. To "swallow up the river that the dragon spewed out of his mouth" means that Pharaoh's evil plot to bring the Hebrew slaves back to Egypt after giving them their freedom was thwarted.

REVELATION 12:17

And the dragon was enraged with the woman, and he went away to make war with the rest of her children, who keep the commandments of God and hold the testimony of Jesus.

Seeing that his attacks are powerless against Jesus, the dragon now turns his attention to the followers of Jesus.

REVELATION 13:1-2

Then I stood on the sand of the seashore. And I saw a beast coming up out of the sea, having ten horns and seven heads. On his horns were ten crowns, and on his heads, blasphe-

The Colosseum, Rome, Italy: Arched entrance (80 in total) into the largest oval amphitheater built by the Flavian dynasty, an iconic majestic symbol of Imperial Rome

MoLarjung / Shutterstock.com

mous names. [2] The beast which I saw was like a leopard, and his feet were like those of a bear, and his mouth was like that of a lion. And the dragon gave him his power, and his throne, and great authority.

The Roman Empire is described as "rising up out of the sea" because Rome was known for her naval power, which dominated all the lands around the Mediterranean sea. The beast in vs. 1 is the same as the great red dragon described in Rev. 12:3. Again, the seven heads of the beast would be the succession of the seven kings of Rome, and the ten horns with crowns upon their heads would be the ten Roman Emperors who followed them, beginning with Julius Caesar and ending with Trajan Caesar. Here again we see that each of Saint John's visions involves some repetition of the other visions.

REVELATION 13:3

And one of his heads looked like it had been fatally wounded; but his fatal wound was healed, and the whole earth marveled at the beast.

Unlike the other six Roman Emperors referenced by the seven heads of the dragon, Emperor Vespasian was a fair and humane leader who did not want to be worshiped as a God. Also, the lack of an heir to the throne of Emperor Nero prior to the installation of Vespasian had temporarily left the Empire in such an unstable state that many thought it might come to an end. That is, the beast had been wounded. Thus, the time period from the death of Nero to the time that Vespasian's son Titus began the siege of Jerusalem was viewed as a temporary wound to the vicious beast.

REVELATION 13:4

And they worshiped the dragon, which gave his power to the beast, and they worshiped the beast, saying, Who is like the beast? Who is able to make war with him?

As previously stated, the dragon represents evil thoughts and worldly aspirations, and the beast represents the enactment of them. We can expect each of Saint John's visions to portray both a general principle and a concrete reference to how that principle would be played out. Accordingly, Chapter 13 begins with a description of the beast as the physical embodiment of the evil that the dragon symbolizes. Verse 2 reads, "...and the dragon gave him [the beast] his power." Thus, vs. 4 continues, "They worshipped the dragon which gave power to the beast: and they worshipped the beast, saying, Who is like the beast? who is able to make war with him?" This part of the vision is a recapitulation of Daniel's second vision, in which the prophet saw four beasts that represented the four dynastic kingdoms—Babylon, Persia, Greece, and Rome. In Daniel's vision, the fourth beast (Rome) is described as "dreadful and terrible" (Dan. 7:7). It had great iron teeth, nails of brass, and was exceedingly strong. This corresponds to Saint John's description of the beast as "like unto a leopard [with feet] as the feet of a bear, and his mouth as the mouth of a lion..." (Rev. 13:2). The power of the beast over all kindreds and nations and tongues (Rev. 13:7) attests to Rome's preeminence in the world at that time. At its height, the Roman Empire stretched from Mesopotamia in the east to the Iberian Peninsula (modern Spain) in the west, and from the Rhine and Danube rivers in the north to the coast of Africa in the south, and had a population of nearly one hundred million people. Daniel further described the beast as being diverse from all the beasts before it; and like Saint John, he described it as having ten horns (Dan. 7:7).

Gladiators of the Colosseum in Rome, Flavian Amphitheatre

David Gonzalez Rebollo / Shutterstock.com

In Daniel 7:16, the prophet Daniel asks how this vision should be interpreted. He is told that all earthly kingdoms would be cast down (metaphorically speaking, the dragon would be cast out of heaven), and the saints of the Most High would possess the kingdom that would rise above all earthly kingdoms. The "kingdom that would rise above all earthly kingdoms" is the kingdom of God, and the "saints of the Most High" who would possess the kingdom are the two-thirds of the angels who were NOT cast out of heaven.

In vs. 20 Daniel is told more about the ten horns of the fourth beast (the Roman Empire). He is told that among the ten horns of the beast, "there came another little horn, before whom there were three of the first horns plucked up by the roots" (Dan. 7:8). A review of Roman history reveals that three of the emperors who preceded the sixth emperor were murdered. These were Julius Caesar, Gaius (Caligula) Caesar, and Claudius Caesar. That means that the "little horn" who followed them would have to be Nero Caesar. In Daniel 7:8 we are further told that in this little horn "were eyes like the eyes of a man, and a mouth speaking great things." Similarly, Saint John tells us that he had "two horns like a lamb and spake like a dragon" (Rev. 13:11), which means that he wielded a combination of religious and political power.

REVELATION 13:5

And there was given to him a mouth speaking boastful and blasphemous things. And power was given to him to make war for forty-two months.

The power given to the beast for forty-two months should not be interpreted as an exact period of time. It is merely a reference to Rome's temporary dynastic influence and the imperial power held by the Roman Emperors.

REVELATION 13:6-7

And he opened his mouth in blasphemy against God, to blaspheme his name, and his temple, and those who dwell in heaven. [7] And he was given authority over every tribe, and people, and nation, and tongue; and it was given to him to make war with the saints, and to overcome them.

Rome blasphemed against God by paying homage to man-made idols rather than the living God. Worse yet, Rome persecuted the saints and ignored their testimony. The ideology of Rome was to conquer all other nations and peoples.

REVELATION 13:8-9

All who dwell on the earth will worship him, everyone whose name has not been written in the book of life of the Lamb slain from the foundation of the world. [9] If anyone has an ear, let him hear.

These verses are spoken to the believers but refer to the unbelievers, who conformed to the evils that the Roman Empire embodied.

REVELATION 13:10

If anyone leads into captivity, he must go into captivity; and if anyone kills with the sword, he must be killed by the sword. Here is the endurance and the faith of the saints.

This is a reminder that we reap what we sow. Evildoers reap the suffering that they sow, and faithful stewards reap the blessings that they sow. However, the saints who were being persecuted by Roman authorities would have to wait patiently, possibly their whole lives, for justice to be served.

Statue relief of emperor Nero's head on the gateway entrance to the park that contains the ruins of his golden palace at domus aurea in Rome

Antony McAulay / Shutterstock.com

Revelation 13:11-12

And I saw another beast coming out of the earth. He had two horns like a lamb, and he spoke like a dragon. [12] He exercises all the authority of the first beast in his presence. And he makes the earth and those who dwell in it to worship the first beast, whose fatal wound was healed.

The phrase, "coming out of the earth" denotes worldliness and earthly pursuits. This second beast is the first beast (Rome) embodied in a man. He demands that the people pay homage to the first beast. Emperor Nero demanded that the people pay homage to Roman authority. That he "spoke like a dragon" meant that he wielded great political power. Here again, we see Saint John portraying the way an attitude or idea played itself out in the social, political, and religious setting of his time.

Revelation 13:13-17

He performs great signs, even being able to make fire come down from heaven onto the earth in the sight of men. [14] Through these signs that he had power to do in front of the beast, he deceives my own people who dwell on the earth, saying to them that they should make an image to the beast who was wounded by the sword and lived. [15] And he had power to give breath to the image of the beast, and to cause as many as would not worship his image to be killed. [16] And he causes all, the small and the great, the rich and the poor, the free and the slave, to receive a mark on their right hands, or on their foreheads; [17] So that no man would be permitted to buy or to sell unless he has that mark, the name of the beast, or the number of his name.

In continuing to describe the beast, Saint John tells us that "He performs great signs, even making fire come down from heaven onto the earth in the sight of men." To "make fire come down from heaven" is a Semitic euphemism that denotes supreme authority. On an historic level, many believe that Emperor Nero, in an effort to make room for the Palatial Complex (a building project for which he could not gain political support) staged the infamous fire that broke out in Rome, and then blamed the disaster on a small religious sect known as "Christians." Subsequently, Nero ruthlessly persecuted the Christians. He had them fed to wild animals during gladiatorial games; he had them crucified; and he set their bodies on fire, using them as human candles in the corridors of his palace. He had the Apostles Peter and Paul put to death, and after attempting to boil the Apostle John in oil, he had him exiled to the island of Patmos. Nero's reputation for sadistic cruelty earned him the nickname "the beast." Recall that in Rev. 13:5 we were told that "there was given unto him (the beast) a mouth speaking great things and blasphemies; and power was given unto him to continue for forty-two months." This accurately describes the reign of Emperor Nero, who spent three-and-a-half years trying to eliminate the early church. In his second letter to the Thessalonians, Saint Paul describes "the son of perdition" as the one who "opposes and exalts himself above all that is called God or that is worshipped; so that he as God sits in the temple, showing himself that he is God" (2 Thess. 3-4). Evidently speaking of the same man, Rev. 13:6 reads, "And he opened his mouth in blasphemy against God, to blaspheme his name, and his tabernacle, and them that dwell in heaven. Nero "blasphemed against God" by declaring himself to be god incarnate. He ordered that all statues in the empire have their heads cut off and replaced with a sculpture of his own head. Nero also wanted an idol of himself to be set up in the Holy Place of the Temple in Jerusalem. All of this was likewise foretold

666 - The number of the beast with the sigil of Lucifer symbol
Afazuddin / Shutterstock.com

by the prophet Daniel, who saw that the beast would "speak great words against the most High, and wear out the saints, and think to change times and laws" (Dan. 7:21, 25).

One of Nero's many legal reforms was to allow no one to buy or sell in the marketplaces without paying homage to the beast. Compliance with this mandate was demonstrated by declaring "Caesar as lord" both in thought and in action (Rev. 13:12). In Rev. 13:16-17 we are told that "he [the beast] causes all, both small and great, rich and poor, free and bond, to receive a mark in their right hand (signifying action), or in their foreheads (signifying thought) and that no man might buy or sell, save he that had the mark, or the name of the beast, or the number of his name."

REVELATION 13:18

Here is wisdom: he who has understanding, let him calculate the number of the beast, for it is the code number of the name of a man. His number is six hundred and sixty-six.

Here Saint John tells us that the number of the beast is the number of a man: his number is 666. Writing in code was common in the biblical days and was used to avoid persecution. The fact that Saint John disguises the name of the beast tells us that he must have been in power at the time that Saint John reduced his vision to writing. Recall that it was Emperor Nero who had banished John to the island of Patmos, where he received the vision. In addition to the name Saint John gives in reference to the beast, Daniel gives us a physical description of the man. We are told that he was "more stout than his fellows" (Dan. 7:20). Caesar Nero had a distinct appearance, so much so that he is specifically described in history as having a thick neck and pot belly, which is consistent with Daniel's description of him. He was certainly also stout in his corrupt ways!

Intuitively one might think that the beast in Saint John's vision will not make his appearance until the end of the age and that his rise to power will be accompanied by extreme depravity on earth. The LORD's disciples felt the same way. In his first letter to the fledgling church, Saint John writes, "Little children, it is the last time: and as ye have heard that the antichrist shall come, even now are there many antichrists; whereby we know that it is the last time" (1 John 2:18). He continues, "And every spirit that confesses not that Jesus Christ is come in the flesh is not of God: and this is that [spirit] of antichrist, whereof ye have heard that it should come; and even now already is in the world" (1 John 4:3). At the time that Saint John wrote these words, the church was under heavy persecution, and John himself was in exile.

Yet it is not surprising that the first-century persecution of the church was not the end, for Jesus had warned that He would return on a day and at an hour that we would not expect; that is, during times of peace and relative tranquility on earth (Matt. 24:36-39). Also, the Revelation of Saint John is far more about the return of Jesus Christ than it is about the coming of the antichrist. Thus, if we are waiting for the appearance of some sort of grand persecution as a sign that the end is near, we may find ourselves caught off guard when the LORD Himself appears! Jesus warned that "if the goodman of the house had known what hour the thief would come, he would have watched, and not suffered his house to be broken through" (Luke 12:39).

In addition, a proper rendering of the book of Revelation clearly shows that the tribulation of the last days will not begin until after the rapture of the church. Only after the LORD's faithful have departed will the metaphorical beast ascend from the bottomless pit to rear his ugly head one last time. Thus, we have no reason to be waiting for the antichrist. What we should be doing is preparing for the LORD Jesus Christ!

REVELATION 14:1

And I saw, and behold, a Lamb standing on Mount Zion, and with him one

Descent of the Holy Spirit - Picture from The Holy Scriptures, Old and New Testaments books collection (1885) Stuttgart-Germany ~ Drawing by Gustave Dore

Courtesy Wikipedia

hundred and forty-four thousand, having his name, and the name of his Father, written on their foreheads.

To have the Father's name "written in their foreheads" means that they had received the Holy Spirit. Beyond that, however, these saints, following the example of Jesus, had learned to live in strict obedience to the Holy Spirit. This unwavering commitment to God made them part of the first resurrection. Again, numbers such as these are not meant to be exact figures; however, the large size of the number tells us that there were a lot of saints, and the two-times multiple of twelve symbolizes their spiritual kinship with the Old Testament (twelve tribes of Israel) and New-Testament (twelve Apostles). The chronology of this vision, as in the others, places the first resurrection between the resurrection of Jesus and His second coming. The fact that there continues to be a stream of fully committed souls implies that the number of those in the first resurrection is growing daily.

Revelation 14:2-5

And I heard a sound from heaven, like the sound of many waters, and like the sound of a great thunder. And I heard the sound of harpists playing on their harps. [3] They sang as it were a new song before the throne, and before the four living creatures and the elders. And no man could learn that song except the one hundred and forty-four thousand who had been redeemed out of the earth. [4] These are those who were not defiled with women, for they are virgins. These are those who follow the Lamb wherever he goes. They were redeemed from among men, the first fruits to God and to the Lamb. [5] In their mouth was found no lie, for they are blameless before the throne of God.

The saints who are part of the first resurrection were fully devoted to God during their lives on earth. The "sound of many waters" is a reference to the praises of the many prophets, saints, martyrs, and confessors of God. The "new song" they are singing is the song of victory over the evils of the world. Their unwavering devotion is the fruit of the Lord's teaching and His sacrifice on the cross, and so the life and resurrection of these saints (and all those who follow them) could be considered the "first-fruits" of the Lord's work. They are the ones who will accompany the Lord and his angels when he returns for His church (Matt. 25:31; 1 Thess. 3:13; Jude 1:14-15). They are also referred to in Rev. 5:3, 5:5, 5:6, 5:8-14, 6:9-11, 14:3, and 20:6. Note that Saint Paul makes no mention of these saints in 1 Cor. 15:23. This is presumably because he had been martyred before Saint John began to share his vision with the growing church.

Revelation 14:6-7

And I saw an angel flying in midst of heaven, having an eternal gospel to proclaim to those who dwell on the earth, and to every nation, tribe, language, and people. [7] And he said with a loud voice, Serve the Lord, and give glory to him; for the hour of his judgment has come. Worship him who made heaven and earth, and the sea, and the springs of waters.

This is a final call to repentance before the second coming of Christ. Repentance is the spiritual act of turning toward God. It involves the surrender of one's own will to God's will, which in turn allows one to turn away from sin and truly worship God. When we obey God, we show that we trust in Him more than in ourselves, and it is this trust, not the

*Saint George and the Dragon, by Raphael, c. 1506,
Italian Renaissance painting, oil on panel. George was patron saint of England*

Everett - Art / Shutterstock.com

works themselves, that guarantees our salvation. Thus, we are not saved by our works, lest any man should boast (Ephes. 2:9). The work through which we are saved was accomplished by Jesus Christ, who, from the foundation of the world, was foreordained to wash our sins away with the blood He would shed on the cross (Rev. 13:8). For this reason, Abraham, who lived before the Ten Commandments and long before the coming of Christ, had the hope of salvation. That hope was consummated when Jesus Christ took our sins upon Himself and was resurrected from the grave. Until then, all those who believed in God had been lying in wait for Jesus to raise them up to eternal life.

REVELATION 14:8

And a second angel followed him, saying, Babylon the great has fallen, that great city which has made all the nations drink of the wine of the passion of her sexual immorality.

The phrase "Babylon is fallen" is in reference to the victory of Jesus Christ and His saints over the evils that ancient Babylon represented.

REVELATION 14:9-10

Then another angel, a third, followed them, saying with a loud voice, If anyone worships the beast and his image, and receives a mark on his forehead or on his hand, [10] he also will drink of the wine of God's wrath, which is mixed with bitterness in the cup of his anger. He will be tormented with fire and sulfur in the presence of the holy angels, and in the presence of the Lamb.

This is a warning to those who think evil thoughts and carry out evil deeds (vs. 9).

REVELATION 14:11

The smoke of their torment goes up forever and ever. They have no rest day or night, those who worship the beast and his image, and whoever receives the mark of his name.

The phrase, "Whoever receives the mark of His name" symbolically means whoever worships and serves the beast or his image.

REVELATION 14:12-13

Here is the perseverance of the saints, those who keep the commandments of God and the faith of Jesus. [13] And I heard a voice from heaven saying, Write, Blessed are the dead who die in the LORD from henceforth. Yes, says the spirit, that they may rest from their labors, for their works will follow them.

Because those who die in the LORD are forgiven of their sins, only their good deeds will be remembered.

REVELATION 14:14-16

And I looked, and behold, a white cloud; and upon the cloud sat one resembling the Son of man, having on his head a golden crown, and in his hand a sharp sickle. [15] And another angel came out of the temple, crying with a loud voice to him who sat on the cloud, Thrust in your sickle and reap; for the harvest of the earth is ripe, and the time has come for you to reap. [16] And he that sat on the cloud thrust in his sickle on the earth, and the earth was harvested.

Last Supper, Carl Bloch ~ Late 19th century
Courtesy of Wikipedia

This is an image of Jesus Christ returning to rapture the church as one harvests the wheat from a field. In so doing, the LORD will separate the wheat from the tears; that is, the believers from the unbelievers (Matt. 3:12).

REVELATION 14:17-20

And another angel came out of the temple which is in heaven. He too had a sharp sickle. [18] Then out of the altar came another angel. He had power over fire, and with a loud voice he cried out to him who had the sharp sickle, saying, Thrust in your sharp sickle and gather the clusters of the vineyards of the earth, for her grapes are fully ripe. [19] And the angel thrust his sickle into the earth and gathered the vintage of the earth, and cast the grapes into the great winepress of the wrath of God. [20] And the winepress was trodden outside of the city until the juice that came out reached even to the bridles of the horses. And the size of the winepress was a thousand and six hundred stadia.

This is the harvest of the tares—the unbelievers. In the biblical days, the winepress was a large basin in which the juice of grapes was expressed by the treading of feet. The use of this image in reference to the damned is symbolic of the ultimate victory of good over evil and points back to Mark 12:36, in which Jesus quotes King David as saying, "The LORD said to my LORD, 'Sit at my right hand until I put your enemies under your feet.'" Also, this occurs "outside the city," indicating that these evildoers were being crushed outside the city of God (i.e., on the earth).

REVELATION 15:1

And I saw another sign in heaven, great and marvelous: seven angels having the seven last plagues; in them is the wrath of God completed.

"Sign in heaven" means a vision of what will happen on earth." The seven last plagues are about to be meted out.

REVELATION 15:2-5

I saw something like a sea of glass mingled with fire, and those who overcame the beast, his image, and the number of his name, standing on the sea of glass, having harps of God. [3] And they were singing the song of Moses, the servant of God, and the song of the Lamb, saying, Great and marvelous are your works, LORD God, the Almighty! Righteous and true are your ways, O King of the nations. [4] Who would not revere you, O LORD, and glorify your name? For you alone are holy. All nations will come and worship you, for your righteous acts have been revealed. [5] And after these things I looked, and behold, the temple of the tabernacle of the testimony in heaven was opened.

While those who are left behind on earth are suffering the tribulation of the last days, those who have ascended to heaven with Christ are glorifying God for their salvation. The "sea of glass" is a reference to the throne of God, as described in Rev. 4:6. Saint John sees all the saved souls standing before the throne worshiping God. The fire represents the Holy Spirit, through which these souls were saved, and the harps in their hands represent the heavenly sound of their praise.

Kiss of Judas. Mosaic in St. Isaac's Cathedral in St. Petersburg by Carl Bryullov
Published in magazine "Niva", publishing house A.F. Marx, St. Petersburg, Russia, 1899

Oleg Golovnev / Shutterstock.com

Revelation 15:6-8

And the seven angels who had the seven last plagues came out of the temple, clothed in linen, pure and fine, and wearing golden sashes around their breasts. [7] And one of the four living creatures gave to the seven angels seven golden bowls full of the wrath of God, who lives forever and ever. [8] The temple was filled with smoke from his glory, and from his power. And no one was able to enter into the temple until the seven plagues of the seven angels would be finished.

The seven angels are summoned out of the temple to unleash the seven last plagues upon the souls who remain on earth after the rapture of the church. This is a reenactment of the wrath that God poured out on Sodom and Gomorrah after Lot and his family had fled the city (Gen. 19:14-28).

Revelation 16:1-2

And I heard a great voice out of the temple saying to the seven angels, Go and pour out the seven bowls of the wrath of God onto the earth. [2] Then the first went, and poured out his bowl onto the earth, and there came a severe and malignant sore upon the people who had the mark of the beast, and upon those who worshiped his image.

Having the "mark of the beast" means that a person is subservient to the beast. That is, they live by the ideals that the beast embodies. Ancient Rome thrived on the ideals of self-centeredness, competition, and the pursuit of personal glory. Those who bought into this mentality were said to have the mark of the beast. They were left behind after the rapture of the church.

Revelation 16:3

And the second angel poured out his bowl into the sea, and it became as the blood of a dead man. And every living soul in the sea died.

The plagues will cause dramatic changes in the climate and ecosystems of the Earth. The overgrowth of an algal species known as Karenia brevis occurs naturally off coasts all over the world and is known as the crimson tide or "red tide." Dead fish wash up on the shore for weeks after the tide has swept through an area.

Revelation 16:4

And the third angel poured out his bowl onto the rivers and springs of water, and they became blood.

The third bowl of wrath refers back to the plagues that God levied upon the Egyptians when Pharaoh refused to let the Hebrews go (Exod. 7:19). Just as He turned the waters to blood then, so will He do during the tribulation of the last days.

Revelation 16:5-6

Then I heard the angel of the waters saying, You are righteous, O Holy One, who is and who was, because you have judged these things. [6] For they shed the blood of the saints and prophets, and you have given them blood to drink, because that is what they deserve.

In his letter to the Galatians, Saint Paul wrote, "Do not be deceived: God is not mocked, for whatever one sows, that will he also reap" (Gal. 6:7). Just as the evildoers shed the blood of the righteous, so too will their blood be shed.

Roman Emperor Titus. 39 CE - 81 CE. From bust at the Ny Carlsberg Glyptotek
Courtesy of Wikipedia

Revelation 16:7-9

And I heard another angel out of the altar saying, Yes, Lord God, the Almighty, true and righteous are your judgments. [8] And the fourth angel poured out his bowl upon the sun, and it was given to him to scorch men with fire. [9] And men were scorched with great heat, and they blasphemed the name of God who has the power over these plagues. And they did not repent to give him glory.

When a star reaches the end of its life, massive explosions cause it to radiate intense light and heat known as a "Supernova." This may occur when the sun, which our nearest star, approaches the end of its life. That those who are caught in this cataclysmic event did not repent is further evidence that the rapture of the church precedes the tribulation if the last days.

Revelation 16:10-11

And the fifth angel poured out his bowl on the throne of the beast, and his kingdom was darkened. And men gnawed their tongues because of the pain; [11] they blasphemed the God of heaven because of their pains and their sores. And they did not repent of their works.

Again we are told that those who are caught in the tribulation of the last days will not repent of their evil works, thus reaffirming that the rapture precedes the tribulation.

Revelation 16:12

And the sixth angel poured out his bowl onto the great river Euphrates. And its water was dried up, that the way might be prepared for the kings of the east.

The drying of the river Euphrates to make way for the kings of the East gives us an image of war breaking out on earth during the tribulation of the last days. This is to be expected for two reasons: first, because all the peacemakers will have been taken out of the world; second, because the proud, knowing that the end is near, will resort to war in defense of fear. In verses 9-11, we were again told that those who are caught in the tribulation of the last days will neither give glory to God nor repent of their evil deeds.

Revelation 16:13

And I saw three unclean spirits, like frogs, coming out of the mouth of the dragon, and out of the mouth of the beast, and out of the mouth of the false prophet.

The unclean spirits that Saint John sees coming out of the mouth of the dragon like frogs represents the spewing out of blasphemous words and evil talk. The dragon we have discussed, and the beast we know; the "false prophet" refers to those who pretend to be pious but inwardly are full of pride and self-centeredness. It may also refer to organized religion, which, like all institutions, is subject to corruption.

Revelation 16:14.

For they are the spirits of devils, working signs and wonders that go forth to the kings of the earth and to the whole world to gather them to the battle of that great day of God Almighty.

This verse refers to the unjust practices and false promises of the rulers of this world. Their sin and corruption will be exposed and brought to an end when The Lord returns.

Revelation 16:15-16

Behold, I come like a thief. Blessed is he who watches and keeps his garments,

Nicolas Poussin's landscape with Saint John on Patmos, 1640

Courtesy of Wikipedia

lest he walk naked and expose his shame. [16] And he gathered them together in the place that in the Hebrew is called Megiddo.

These verses symbolize 1) the LORD returning when the world least expects Him; and 2) the last battle that will be fought on earth: Almighty God and his followers versus those who are left behind after the rapture. Symbolically, this battle will be fought on the plains of Megiddo, for it was there that the chosen people of God, the Hebrew people, had won many battles against their enemies under God's guidance and protection. We know that this battle cannot literal because the Lord and His followers are peacemakers. Moreover, the battle will be fought after the rapture of the church. Verses 9, 11, and 21 make this clear, as they emphasize that even in the midst of the various plagues that will break out on earth during the tribulation of the last days, none of the inhabitants of the earth will repent of their evil deeds. When the L ORD returns for His church, He will leave behind those who He knows will never repent.

Note that the events portrayed in each of Saint John's visions up to this point occur in exactly the same order. Through this consistency, it is crystal clear that the "great tribulation" is a past event and that the tribulation of the last days will not begin until after the rapture of the church.

REVELATION 16:17-21

And the seventh angel poured out his bowl into the air. And a loud voice came out of the temple of heaven, from the throne, saying, It is finished! [18] And there were lightnings, and sounds, and thunders; and there was a great earthquake, the likes of which there has never been from the time that there were men on the earth, so great an earthquake, so mighty. [19] And the great city was divided into three parts, and the cities of the nations fell. Babylon the great was remembered in the sight of God, to give to her the cup of the wine of the fierceness of his wrath. [20] And every island fled away, and the mountains were found no more. [21] And great hailstones, about the size of a talent, fell out of the sky onto the people. And they blasphemed God because of the plague of the hail, for the plague was exceedingly severe.

These cataclysmic events will mark the end of the age and the end of the universe as we know it. In the second letter of Saint Peter, we read, "But the day of the LORD will come as a thief in the night; in the which the heavens will pass away with a great noise, and the elements will melt with fervent heat, the earth also and the works that are therein will be burned up" (2 Peter 3:10).

The Fifth Prophetic Vision

REVELATION 17:1-10

Then one of the seven angels who had the seven bowls came and talked to me, saying, Come, I will show you the judgment of the great prostitute who sits upon many waters, [2] With whom the kings of the earth committed adultery, and those who dwell on the earth have been made drunk with the wine of her sexual immorality. [3] And he carried me away in the spirit into the wilderness. And I saw a woman sitting on a

Tower of Babel as religious concept

Elena Schweitzer/ Shutterstock.com

scarlet-colored beast, full of blasphemous names, having seven heads and ten horns. [4] The woman was dressed in purple and scarlet, and decked with gold and precious stones and pearls, having in her hand a golden cup full of the abominations and impurities of her sexual immorality. [5] On her forehead was written a name that not all could understand: BABYLON THE GREAT, THE MOTHER OF HARLOTS AND THE ABOMINATIONS OF THE EARTH. [6] And I saw that the woman was drunk with the blood of the saints and with the blood of the martyrs of Jesus. And when I saw her, I wondered with great amazement. [7] And the angel said to me, Why do you marvel? I will tell you the mystery of the woman, and of the beast that carries her, which has the seven heads and the ten horns. [8] The beast that you saw was, and is not, and is ready to come up from the bottomless pit and to go into destruction. Those who dwell on the earth and whose names are not written in the book of life from the foundation of the world will marvel when they see the beast that was, and is not, and now whose end has come. [9] Here is wisdom. The seven heads are seven mountains on which the woman sits. [10] And there are seven kings, of whom five have fallen, one is, the other has not yet come. And when he comes, he must continue for a short pace.

Revelations from God can only be perceived through the lens of the Holy Spirit. Hence the phrase, "He carried me away in the spirit" (vs. 3) indicates that the Revelator is about to relate another vision. Time-wise, this fifth prophetic vision begins with the battle waged by Jesus against the false beliefs and idolatry of the beast. Here the beast represents the evils of the world. The whore that sits upon many waters is a reference to ancient Babylon, which was built at the junction of what were considered the two great bodies of water at the time—the Tigris and Euphrates rivers. Until the rise of the British Empire in the seventeenth century, Babylon, Damascus, and other ancient cities were known as central markets for cloth, jewelry, spices, and other luxuries. Their warehouses were filled with diverse goods and delicacies that were transported on cargo ships and the backs of camels. The Babylonians also practiced slave trade, which turned human beings into material commodities. Besides their excessive materialism, the people of Babylon were unfair in their trade practices, and the kings of Babylon were unfair in their war practices. In light of this, the prophets often referred to Babylon as the prototypic example of vanity, moral depravity, and political corruption.

The choice of the word "fornicated" to describe Babylon deserves special attention. Normally, sexual intimacy is based on a marital commitment. What makes fornication sinful is that there is sexual intimacy without a lifelong commitment. This defrauds the partner. Through their unjust practices, the Babylonians had defrauded their neighbors. Thus, they were said to have fornicated. Those with whom they traded were made drunk with the wine of their fornication in that they were so caught up in materialism that they could not see that they were being cheated. The ancient Aramaic word for Babylon is "babel," which means "confusion." The deceitfulness of the Babylonians made Babylon a land of confusion. Babylon is also the place where the confounding of language divided the people of the earth after they attempted to build a tower to establish their imagined in-dependence from God (Gen. 11:4-9). Like the confounding of language, the fall of Babylon exemplified that which would inevitably happen to all corrupt peoples, leaders, and governments.

Entry of Alexander the Great into Babylon. A 1665 painting by Charles LeBrun
Courtesy Wikipedia

In verse 3 the sexual metaphor continues with the prostitute sitting on the beast, who is her partner in sin. Here, the seven heads of the beast are seven kingdoms. In verse 9 they are referred to as "seven mountains" because of their preeminence on the landscape of world history. In Jeremiah 51:25, the Babylonian Empire is referred to as a mountain. The seven kings are the leaders of these mountain kingdoms. They are: Egypt, Assyria, Babylon, Persia, Greece, Rome, and the Ottoman Empire. In verse 10 we are told, "five are fallen and one is." At the time of Saint John's vision, five had fallen, and the one that stood was, of course, the Roman Empire. The one that was to come was the Ottoman Empire. The Turkish-Ottomans were the last and one of the largest political structures that the western world had known since the fall of the Roman Empire. Notably, the Ottomans also occupied the same region of the world as the other dynasties in Saint John's vision.

Thus, what Saint John sees in his fifth prophetic vision is a picture of the kingdoms of the world (symbolized by the scarlet-colored beast) submitting to the evil ideology of the "mother of harlots and abominations of the earth" (symbolized by Babylon the Great). The incestuous relationship between the harlot and the beast is symbolic of the fact that all the kingdoms of this world share the same sinful practices, including the persecution of God's faithful servants (vs. 6).

The immoral sexual image presented here could also be seen as a reference to the relationship between the lewd Emperor Titus and the lascivious Jewish princess Berenice, who was the sister of Herod Agrippa and the mistress of Titus. Berenice was referred to by some as "the whore of Babylon" and "the new Cleopatra, while Titus was a blasphemous leader who wanted to be worshiped as a God.

The beast that "was, and is not," is a reference to the fleeting power of evil. The life, death, and resurrection of Jesus Christ had defeated the forces of evil and ushered in the thousand-year reign of Christ (Rev. 20:6; 1 Cor. 15:25; Acts 2:17-19; 3:20,21; John 18:36). But at the end of the thousand years, the LORD will return for His faithful servants. In his first letter to the Corinthians, Saint Paul writes: "For he must reign till he has put all [His] enemies under his feet. And the last enemy that shall be destroyed is death" (1 Cor. 15:25-26). The same is written in the Psalms (Ps. 110:1-2). Saint Paul then goes on to tell us when death will be destroyed: it will be destroyed "when this corruptible shall have put on incorruption, and this mortal shall have put on immortality" (1 Cor. 15:54). That is, at the resurrection of the just, when they meet the Lord in the air (1 Thess. 4:16-17). After that, those who remain on the earth will be stricken with terror as they experience the unrestrained forces of evil. This is referred to metaphorically as the loosening of the dragon from the bottomless pit for a short time (Rev. 20:2-3). The dragon, who is the devil and Satan, will be loosed in the sense that the thousand-year reign of Christ will have ended, and his time will be short in the sense that the period between the rapture of the church and the end of the world will be relatively brief.

REVELATION 17:11-14

And the beast that was, and is not, even he is the eighth, and is of the seven; and he is destined to be destroyed. [12] The ten horns that you saw are ten kings who have received no kingdom as yet, but they receive authority as kings for one hour with the beast. [13] These have one mind, and they give their power and authority to the beast. [14] These will war against the Lamb, and the Lamb will overcome them, for he is LORD of lords, and King of kings, and those who are with him are called chosen and faithful.

The Destruction of Leviathan (1865) by Gustave Dore
Courtesy Wikipedia

The symbolism used here does not refer to a specific political or religious entity but to the evil principles that the kingdoms of this world embody. The beast that "was, and is not," who is referred to as being "of the seven"...is evil itself, which will ultimately be overcome by the King of kings and Lord of lords Jesus Christ.

Revelation 17:15

Then he said to me, The waters which you saw, where the prostitute sits, are multitudes of people and races and nations and languages.

The image of the whore sitting upon many waters is a reference to the subservice of the masses to the dictates of sin and idolatry. Elsewhere in the Bible, water is used to represent the masses. In Daniel 7:3 we read, "and four great beasts came up from the sea." Likewise, in Revelation 20:13 we read, "and the sea gave up the dead which were in it." Thus, the images of water and the sea represent the masses.

Revelation 17:16

The ten horns which you saw, and the beast, these will hate the harlot, and will make her desolate, and will make her naked, and will eat her flesh, and will burn her with fire.

Though the whore and the beast are pictured as a unified incestuous pairing, they turn against each other because evil destroys itself. When people use one another, they ultimately hurt one another. Wrongdoing never works out for anyone's good because a self-centered attitude destroys the soul and divides the people. This is not to be confused with the question that Jesus posed to the Pharisees when He asked, "How can Satan cast out Satan?" (Matt. 12:26). In that case, Jesus was not referring to the divisiveness of evil; He was simply saying that good deeds could not be the work of the devil.

Revelation 17:17

For God has put it in their hearts to do his will, and to be of one mind, and to give their kingdom to the beast until the words of God should be fulfilled.

"God shall put it in their hearts to do his will" is a reference to God's ultimate authority. It is an ancient Semitic manner of speaking in which everything, including man's own folly, was attributable to God because God gives us the freedom to choose. For example, in the book of Isaiah we read, "I form the light, and create darkness. I make peace, and create evil. I the Lord do all of these things" (Isa. 45:7). Clearly, God is not the author of evil, and He does not create darkness. God is love and light. However, God might choose to allow evil to exist for a time. In the book of Exodus we are told that God "hardened Pharaoh's heart" against Moses and the Hebrew slaves (Exodus 7:13). This does not mean that God forced Pharaoh to be stubborn. Pharaoh was stubborn of his own free will, and out of respect for his freedom to choose, God allowed him to be that way. All of us should take this as a solemn warning: if we stubbornly refuse to obey God, what happened to Pharaoh might happen to us.

Revelation 18:1-3

After these things, I saw another angel coming down out of heaven, having great authority; and the earth was illuminated with his glory. [2] He cried with a mighty voice, saying, Fallen, fallen is Babylon the great; she has become a habitation of those possessed by devils; a shelter of every unclean spirit, of every unclean and detestable bird, of every unclean and loathsome beast. [3] For the kings of the earth have committed fornication with her, and all the na-

Ink hand drawn sketch in old engraving style
ArtMari/ Shutterstock.com

tions of the earth have drunk the wine of her wrath, and the merchants of the earth have grown rich through the abundance of her delicacies.

The phrase, I saw another angel come down from heaven" means that Saint John is about to receive more of this prophetic vision. As previously discussed, the word "angel" means messenger. That the earth was "lighted with his glory" means that the message the angel is about to convey has great power and significance. In this case, the angel bears the word of judgment against the evil that ancient Babylon embodied. As is customary in the book of Revelation, the spiritual principle that is revealed also has a practical application within the culture and times in which the revelation was received. Here we are told that Babylon and all those who traded with her were under the same condemnation because all of them were in collusion.

REVELATION 18:4

And I heard another voice from heaven, saying, Come out of her, my people, that you may have no part in her sins, and that you do not receive of her plagues.

Here we have a clear picture of the rapture of the church occurring before the start of the tribulation of the last days. In verse 4 we read, "Come out of her, my people, that ye be not partakers of her sins, and that ye receive not of her plagues." Again Babylon is being used as the prototypical symbol of all the evils of the world, and the church is being called out of her.

REVELATION 18:5-7

For her sins have reached to heaven, and God has remembered her iniquities. [6] Return to her just as she returned to you, and repay her double what her works deserve. In the cup that she mixed, mix her a double portion. [7] As much as she has glorified herself and lived deliciously, so much give her suffering and sorrow. For she says in her heart, I sit as a queen, and am no widow, and will in no way see mourning.

God's patience has been exhausted, and the day of His wrath has arrived! Now, with the elect having already been taken up to heaven with Jesus Christ, the judgment of God is ready impose itself on the world like a thief in the night" (vs. 8).

REVELATION 18:8-19

Therefore in one day her plagues will come: death, mourning, and famine; and she will be utterly burned with fire; for mighty is the LORD God, and He is the one who judges her. [9] The kings of the earth who committed sexual immorality and lived wantonly with her will weep and wail over her when they see the smoke of her burning. [10] They will stand far off for the fear of her torment, saying, Woe, woe, that great city, Babylon, that great city! For in one hour your judgment came, and you have been condemned. [11] And the merchants of the earth will weep over her and mourn over her, for no man buys from her anymore. [12] Never again will there be merchandise of gold, silver, precious stones, pearls, fine linen, silk, scarlet, vessels of ivory, vessels of most precious wood, and of brass, and iron, and marble, [13] and cinnamon, incense, perfume, frankincense, wine, olive oil, flour, wheat, sheep, hides, horses, chariots, and slaves. [14] The

Penitent by Niccolo Frangipane, 1574
Courtesy of Wikipedia

fruits which your soul lusted after have been lost to you, and all things that were dainty and sumptuous have perished from you, and you will find them no more, no more at all. [15] The merchants of these things, who were made rich by her, will stand far away for the fear of her torment, and they will weep and mourn; [16] saying, Woe, woe, that great city, she who was dressed in fine linen, purple, and scarlet, and decked with gold and precious stones and pearls. For in one hour such great riches and precious things are lost! [17] And every shipmaster, and every mariner, and every man who labors at sea stood far off, [18] and cried out when they looked upon the smoke of her burning, saying, What city is like this great city? [19] And they cast dust on their heads, and cried, weeping and mourning, saying, Woe, woe, that great city, through which all who had their ships in the sea were made rich by reason of her great wealth. For in one hour she is made desolate.

These verses describe what is about to befall those who are left behind. All earthly kingdoms and rulers will be destroyed along with their wicked ways. Those who would not be killed immediately by the plagues would marvel at the swiftness and severity of the calamity that will be occurring. That they would "cast dust on their heads" (vs. 19) is not meant to imply true repentance but rather intense frustration and remorse over having been deceived by the temptations of the world. To this day, neareasterners throw dirt on their heads and in their faces as an expression of intense regret and remorse. Because these damned souls are so hard of hart, they will not repent; instead, they will become even more callous and enraged in response to their misery. Recall that in vs. 9:20 of Saint John's fourth prophetic vision, as in this vision, we are told that those who had not yet been killed by the plagues "repented not of the works of their hands."

Revelation 18:20

Rejoice over her, O heaven, you saints, apostles, and prophets; for God has avenged you on her.

God's faithful servants are told to rejoice over His faithfulness to them and commitment to His word in avenging worldly injustice.

Revelation 18:21-23

And a mighty angel took up a stone like a great millstone and cast it into the sea, saying, Babylon, that great city, shall be violently overthrown and will be found no more at all. [22] And the sound of harpists, and minstrels, and flute players, and trumpeters will be heard no more at all in you. And craftsman, of whatever craft, will not be found any more in you. And the sound of a mill will be heard no more at all in you. [23] And the light of a candle will shine no more at all in you. The voice of the bridegroom and of the bride will be heard no more at all in you; for your merchants were the princes of the earth, and by your sorceries were all nations deceived.

These verses emphasize the swiftness, severity, and completeness of the destruction of the tribulation of the last days.

A depiction of the Raising of the Cross, by Sebastiano Mazzoni, 17th century, Ca' Rezzonico
Courtesy of Wikipedia

REVELATION 19:1-10

After these things I heard something like a loud voice of a great multitude in heaven, saying, Hallelujah! Salvation, power, and glory belong to our God. [2] For true and righteous are his judgments. He has judged the great harlot who corrupted the earth with her sexual immorality, and he has avenged the blood of his servants at her hand. [3] And a second time they said, Hallelujah! Her smoke goes up forever and ever. [4] And the twenty-four elders and the four living creatures fell down and worshiped God, saying to him who sits on the throne, Amen, Hallelujah! [5] And a voice came from the throne, saying, Give praise to our God, all you his servants, you who fear him, both small and the great! [6] And I heard something like the voice of a great multitude, and like the voice of many waters, and like the sound of mighty thunders, saying, Hallelujah! For the LORD our God, the Almighty, reigns! [7] Let us rejoice and be exceedingly glad, and give glory to him. For the marriage feast of the Lamb has come, and his bride has made herself ready. [8] And it was given to her that she should be arrayed in fine linen, pure and white: for the fine linen is the righteousness of the saints. [9] And he said to me, Write, Blessed are those who are invited to the marriage supper of the Lamb. Then He said to me, These are true words of God. [10] And I fell down before his feet to worship him; but he said to me, Do not do that, for I am a fellow servant with you and with your brothers who hold the testimony of Jesus. Worship God, for the testimony of Jesus is the spirit of Prophecy.

Note again that in this fifth prophetic vision, the bride of Christ (the church) is safely gathered together in the abode of God while the tribulation of the last days is taking place on earth. In verses 2 and 3, the LORD fulfills His promise to punish the wicked and avenge the blood of the martyrs. The faithful are rejoicing both because they are with the LORD and because they see how He kept His word to bring peace to the faithful and judgment to those who persecuted them on earth. That "her smoke rose up forever and ever" means that the punishment of the damned will be eternal.

Note that the eternal punishment of the damned and the eternal rewards of the faithful are what make these consequences real. Were they not eternal, they would merely equate to a dream; for what is a dream other than that which comes to an end? Experiences in the night are a dream because they come to an end, and life on earth is a dream because it too comes to an end. However, the thoughts and deeds of the heart have eternal consequences because the soul is eternal. Therefore, we should never allow the circumstances of our lives prevent us from making moral choices.

Another way of understanding eternal punishments and rewards is as follows. If the Lord were to punish our bad deeds or, conversely, reward our good deeds for a limited period of time, then what would happen next? Would rewards and punishments come to an end? Such a thing would not square up with the fact that the soul is eternal. Therefore, rewards and punishments are necessarily eternal.

Yet another way of understanding eternal punishments and rewards is to recognize that life, both here on earth and in the hereafter, is lived in the present. Therefore, there really is no time either here or there except for what we agree to call "time." Hence, rewards and punishments are eternal even though specific circumstances on earth are temporal.

Finally, we must remember that God Himself is eternal. Hence, obedience to God has eternal

Painting of St. John the evangelist in church Santa Maria della Salute by Antonio Triva da Reggio (1626 - 1699)

Renata Sedmakova / Shutterstock.com

consequences, and disobedience to God has eternal consequences. The faithful will be with God forever in heaven, whereas the unfaithful will be separated from God forever in hell.

In verse 19:4, note again the distinction between the "twenty-four elders" and the rest of the saved souls referred to in verse 5. Those who had been part of the first resurrection are gathered around the altar, whereas those who were caught up with Christ in the rapture are in the congregation. This parallels the mass on earth, during which we see the priest, who represents Jesus Christ, surrounded by the deacons, who represent the four and twenty elders. This same parallel is seen between the physical structure of the Old City of Jerusalem with its twelve gates and the New Jerusalem described in Revelation 21:12-25. It is also seen in the many parallels between life on earth and life in heaven.

The Sixth Prophetic Vision

REVELATION 19:11

I saw the heaven opened, and behold, a white horse, and he who sat on it is called Faithful and True. In righteousness he judges and makes war.

The phrase "I saw the heaven opened" means that Saint John is about to receive another vision from God. Unlike the previous visions, which include the events leading up to the rapture of the church, this sixth vision is abbreviated; it begins with the promised return of Jesus Christ, but the chronology of events is the same as in all the other visions.

REVELATION 19:12-13

His eyes were like a flame of fire, and on his head were many crowns. And he had a name written, that no man knew but he himself. [13] And he was clothed with a garment sprinkled with blood. And he called his name, The Word of God.

"Eyes like a flame of fire" symbolizes the power, omniscience, and burning love of Jesus Christ. The garment sprinkled with blood is symbolic of the blood that Jesus shed for us on the cross. The name that no man knew is "I AM THAT I AM," as the LORD told Moses on Mount Horeb (Exodus 3:14). The "many crowns on His head" refer to the LORD's kingship and the crowns He gives to those who serve Him faithfully. This is also a parallel description: Jesus and His disciples wearing crowns of victory just as the dragon and his disciples wore crowns of destruction.

REVELATION 19:14

The armies that were in heaven followed him on white horses, clothed in fine linen, pure and white.

Here is a picture of Jesus Christ returning with all His angels and saints. The saints who follow Him are the same ones who were present at the marriage supper of the Lamb described in the previous vision (Rev. 19:8). They are the elders who were gathered around the throne of God clothed in white garments (Rev. 4:4). Their return with Jesus (Jude 1:14) tells us that there are resurrected souls who reign with Christ in heaven prior to the resurrection of the just and the rapture of the church (Rev. 20:4). They are part of the "first resurrection," which is referred to again in Rev. 20:5. These saints will, along with Jesus, also judge the twelve tribes of Isreal after the general resurrection (Matt. 19:28; Luke 22:28-30). "Garments of fine linen, pure and white" denote the chastity and purity of these saints (Rev. 3:4-6). They were made clean by cleansing themselves with the blood of Jesus Christ. No one can enter

Painting of Pieta (Madonna of Seven Sorrows) in church Chiesa die Cappuchini by unknown artist of 17th century

Renata Sedmakova / Shutterstock.com

the abode of God without being washed clean of all their sins and cleansed of all their iniquity through the Lord's atoning sacrifice on the cross (Rev. 3:18; 21:27).

REVELATION 19:15-16

And out of his mouth came a sharp two-edged sword, that with it he should strike the nations and rule them with a rod of iron. He will tread the winepress of the fierceness of the wrath of Almighty God. [16] And he had on his garment and on his thigh a name written, KING OF KINGS, AND LORD OF LORDS.

A sword is symbolic of war, and a sharp blade divides parts that would otherwise be hard to separate. The word of God makes war against the corruption of the world and draws a distinction between that which is right and that which is wrong. Jesus is depicted as ruling the world with a rod of iron because, in the biblical days, iron was the strongest metal available. An ancient winepress had two parts: an upper trough, in which grapes were trodden under foot, and a lower trough into which the juice flowed. The image of Jesus "treading the winepress" is symbolic of the crushing victory that He would have over the sin and corruption of this world (1 Cor. 15:27).

REVELATION 19:17-18

And I saw an angel standing in the sun. He cried with a loud voice, saying to all the birds of the air, Come and gather together for the great supper of God. [18] That you may eat the flesh of kings, the flesh of captains, the flesh of mighty men, the flesh of horses and of those who sit on them, and the flesh of all men, both free and slave, both small and great.

Again, the word "angel" means "messenger." Angels are the messengers of God's word and loving protection. "Standing in the sun" means that God's word would be spoken openly and that whatever was hidden would be revealed. The darkness hides things, but the sun exposes things. Jesus said, "There is nothing hidden that will not be revealed" (Luke 12:2). The sun is also symbolic of God, light, and truth. When the truth is revealed, the proud will be brought to nothing, and the birds of the air (the saved souls) will enjoy spiritual victory over them. Like the dead animals that become food for the vultures, the damned will be judged by the righteous (Matthew 19:28; 1 Corinthians 6:2). That all the unbelievers would be consumed, "both small and great," is symbolic of the fact that God is impartial, showing no favoritism to worldly status or position.

REVELATION 19:19

Then I saw the beast and the kings of the earth and their armies gathered together to make war against him who sat on the horse, and against his armies.

In this verse, those who remain on earth are depicted as making war with God because they refused to surrender their lives to Him. This is described as the battle of Armageddon because it was on the plains of Megiddo that God's chosen people, the Hebrews, had, under God's protection, won most of the battles they fought against hostile tribes and warring factions. Jesus is pictured as returning on a white horse because in the East, white stands for purity, virtue, and righteousness.

REVELATION 19:20

And the beast was taken, and with him the false prophet who, by working signs and wonders in his sight, deceived those who had received the mark of the beast and who worshiped his image. These

Saint John the Evangelist painting, Vienna

Sedmak / 123rf.com

two were thrown alive into the lake of fire, which burns with sulfur.*

Here we see the light of truth exposing all the lies of the beast and the deception of the false prophet. The "false prophet" is a reference to anything that is false, misleading, or deceiving. That includes false religions and corrupt ideologies, of which their were many during the time that Saint John received his visions.

REVELATION 19:21

The rest were killed by the sword that came out of the mouth of him who sat on the horse. And all the birds were filled with their flesh.

The sword of Him who sat upon the white horse is the word of God, which proceeds from the mouth of the One who is sitting on the white horse–Jesus Christ. God's word is pictured as an instrument that cuts to the truth and exposes all lies and deception.

The Seventh Prophetic Vision

REVELATION 20:1-4

I saw an angel coming down out of heaven, having the key to the bottomless pit and a great chain in his hand. [2] And he seized the dragon, that old serpent, which is the devil and Satan, who deceives the whole world, and bound him for a thousand years, [3] and cast him into the abyss, and shut it up, and sealed it over him, that he should no more deceive the nations until the thousand years should pass. After this, he will be loosed for a short time. [4] And I saw thrones, and those who sat on them, and judgment was given to them. And I saw the souls of those who had been beheaded for the testimony of Jesus, and for the word of God, and who did not worship the beast or his image, and did not receive his mark upon their forehead or on their hand. They lived and reigned with Christ for a thousand years.

Here, the angel that Saint John sees coming down from heaven represents three things: 1) the start of another prophetic vision; 2) the power of the word of God; and 3) the life, death, and resurrection of Jesus Christ. It was the ministry of Jesus and the power of the Holy Spirit that seized the dragon and sealed him in a bottomless pit. The thousand years of the dragon's confinement refers to the church age, which is the period of time between the resurrection of Jesus and the rapture of the church. Again, "one thousand" is not meant to signify an exact period of time. Let us recall that for the LORD, "a day is like a thousand years, and a thousand years are like a day" (2 Peter 3:8). What's more, the LORD told us that no one knows the day or the hour when He will return (Matt. 24:36).

During the thousand-year reign of Christ, the Holy Spirit would work through the life, death, and resurrection of Jesus to confront and denounce evil in the world. The thousand years is the age when the devil's dominion would be restrained by the light of Christ. As was spoken by the prophet Joel, "And it shall come to pass afterward, [that] I will pour out my spirit upon all flesh; and your sons and your daughters shall prophesy, your old men shall dream dreams, your young men shall see visions: and also upon the servants and upon the handmaids in those days will I pour out my spirit. And I will shew wonders

The Resurrection of Jesus Christ

in the heavens and in the earth, blood, and fire, and pillars of smoke. The sun shall be turned into darkness, and the moon into blood, before the great and the terrible day of the LORD comes. And it shall come to pass, [that] whosoever shall call on the name of the LORD shall be delivered: for in mount Zion and in Jerusalem shall be deliverance, as the LORD hath said, and in the remnant whom the LORD shall call" (Joel 2:28-32; Acts 2:17).

By exposing the truth, Jesus Christ prevented falsehood, sin, and corruption from continuing to deceive the nations. However, after the rapture of the church, the spirit of truth together with the LORD's faithful servants will have been taken out of the world, thus releasing the dragon for a short time. That "short time" refers to the tribulation of the last days, which will be relatively brief due to the severity of God's judgment.

Again, each of Saint John's visions describe the events to come in the same chronological order. If this were not so, we would not be able to decipher the order of events, and the prophesy would lose some of its value. Note that the prophet Joel, writing nearly ten centuries before Saint John received the Revelation of Jesus Christ, foretells the same order of events as the Revelation.

At this point in the seventh prophetic vision, the rapture of the church has not yet occurred, and yet Saint John sees thrones and judgment given to those who are on the thrones. He then tells us who is seated on the thrones: they are again the LORD's faithful servants—the martyrs who are part of the first resurrection. They are the ones who did not receive the mark of the beast on their foreheads or on their hands; that is, they refused to think like the beast or act like the beast. Jesus promised that these faithful servants would sit on thrones and judge the twelve tribes of Israel (Matt. 19:28; Luke 22:30). The "twelve tribes of Israel" refers not only to the Jews but to all those who will be caught up with Christ at His second coming; they are God's spiritual Israel (Gal. 6:16). These will be judged not for their sins, for their names are written in the Lamb's book of life (vs. 12). Rather, they will be judged for their good deeds. Of course, the rest of the dead will be judged as well, but they will be judged for their sins because they rejected the atoning blood of Jesus Christ (Matt. 25:31; 1 Cor. 6:2).

This vision further indicates that those who reign with Christ in heaven are not just with Him spiritually; they are with Him in body as well. Like Jesus, they are part of the "first resurrection." The term "resurrection" refers to the rejoining of the physical body to the spiritual body as demonstrated by Jesus after He rose from the grave (Luke 24:36-43). This is the only way that the term "resurrection" is used in the Bible. Also, if the term were referring to a spiritual rebirth, the Revelator would not be able to say that the second death, which is spiritual death, has no power over those in the first resurrection because until we die physically, all of us are at risk of falling away spiritually (Rev. 2:10-11; 20:6; Matt 10:22).

In Matt. 28:2, we are told that when Jesus was resurrected, there was a great earthquake, and the angel of the LORD rolled back the stone of the tomb. The reason the stone was rolled back was not to permit Jesus to leave the tomb. Rather, it was to allow his disciples to enter the tomb and see that His body was gone (Matt. 28:5-6). We know from the gospel of John that the resurrected Jesus was able to pass through walls (John 20:26). Hence, He had no need for the stone to be rolled back when it was time for Him to leave the tomb. The stone was rolled back to allow His disciples to see that Jesus had been resurrected!

The same applies to the opening of the tombs of the saints. In Matt. 27 we are told that while Jesus was hanging on the cross, the tombs of many of the saints were opened. Note, however, that they were not seen by anyone until after Jesus Himself was resurrected (Matt. 27:50-53). This suggests that their emergence from their tombs was something more than what had happened to Lazarus and others who Jesus had raised from the dead. Those individuals eventually died again (1 Kings 17:17-24; 2 Kings 4:31-37; 13:20-21; Luke 7:14-15; 8:49-55; John 11:21-44). In contrast, these

Resurrection of Christ, old fresco
Nattesha / Shutterstock.com

saints appear to have participated in what had happened to the LORD Himself; they were raised in an imperishable body just as Jesus had been. This is further suggested by the fact that their bones had vanished from their graves just as Jesus's body had vanished from His grave (Matt. 27: 52-53). Also like Jesus, these resurrected saints appeared to many in Jerusalem (Matt. 27:53). The "many" to whom they appeared were other believers; unbelievers could not see them. Recall that Jesus had told His disciples that after His resurrection only the believers would see Him (John 14:19). He told them that heavenly things could be seen only through the eyes of the Holy Spirit (John 3:3; 19:38-39). The resurrected Jesus and the resurrected saints were part of "heavenly things"; hence, they could be seen only by those who had received the Holy Spirit. This is consistent with the way that their sightings were described. The Bible says that Jesus and the resurrected saints "appeared" to the believers in different places. The word "appeared" has a distinct meaning; it is used in the Bible only when God, a departed soul, or an angel comes from the other side to briefly visit those who are still in the world (Gen. 12:7; Judges 13:9-10; Matt. 1:20; Matt.16:9; 16:12; 16:14; Mark 9:4; Luke 1:11; 22:43). Like Jesus, these resurrected saints were moving back and forth between earthly life and heavenly life. They were going wherever their LORD was going (Rev. 14:4; John 20:17-19). Thus, it appears that their tombs had been opened not to allow them to exit but to allow those who would later see them to verify that they had been resurrected! Their resurrection immediately after the LORD's resurrection was a demonstration of the Lord's eagerness to share His victory with them.

However, as suggested by Saint John's vision, there appears to be a growing number of "big saints" who are part of the first resurrection. If, however, the bodies of these saints were to disappear from their tombs, it could lead to claims that their remains were stolen. Even the body of Jesus, whose tomb was sealed and heavily guarded, was thought by some to have been stolen after His resurrection. Of course, such claims were silenced by the fact that He (and the resurrected saints who followed Him) appeared to many! In this case, however, there was a great advantage—even necessity—for their bodies be absent from the tomb. This is in contrast to the resurrected saints of today who, short of appearing to many, would need some way of demonstrating their glorified status. Thus, it is possible that those saints whose bodies remain incorrupt, such as Saint Vincent de Paul, Saint Bernadette Soubirous, and Saint Catherine of Siena, are actually part of the first resurrection. Their incorrupt state may be God's way of revealing that they are in heaven reigning with Christ.

REVELATION 20:5

This is the first resurrection. The rest of the dead lived not again until the thousand years were finished.

This verse clearly indicates two things: 1) that those in the first resurrection precede the rapture in their ascent to heaven; and 2) that the rapture of the church marks the end of the thousand-year reign of Christ. Note, however, that the Apostle Paul, in describing the second resurrection in his letter to the Corinthians, makes no mention of the dead who are NOT in Christ (1 Cor. 15:52). These lost souls are presumably resurrected at the end of the world along with those who die in the tribulation of the last days.

REVELATION 20:6

Blessed and holy is he who has part in the first resurrection. Over these the second death has no power, but they will be priests of God and of Christ, and will reign with him a thousand years.

The second death, which is spiritual death, has no power over those in the first resurrection because

Saints and Martyrs, by Fra Angelico
Courtesy of Wikipedia

they have already been judged worthy to reign with Christ in heaven.

Revelation 20:7

And after the thousand years have past, Satan will be released from his prison.

The thousand-year reign of Christ will end with the rapture of the church and the resurrection of the just. Then, with the world devoid of all that is good, total chaos and will break out everywhere on earth. In other words, Satan will be released from his prison.

Revelation 20:8-9

And he will come out to deceive the nations which are in the four corners of the earth, even to China and Mongolia, to gather them together for war, the number of whom is as the sand of the sea. [9] And they went up over the plain of the earth, and surrounded the camp of the saints and the beloved city. And fire came down from God out of heaven and consumed them.

After the rapture of the church, war will break out on earth because the devil will be on the loose and will have unrestrained influence over people. With every godly person having been taken out of the world, it will be total pandemonium. The violence that will erupt is depicted as a battle against God and His saints because the inhabitants of the earth will burn with anger against them and desperately try to reject the fact that their time is short.

Revelation 20:10

And the devil who deceived them was thrown into the lake of fire and sulfur, where are also the beast and the false prophet; they will be tormented day and night forever and ever.

All evil will be destroyed physically and spiritually when God pours out His wrath upon the earth (Rev. 16:1).

Revelation 20:11-13

And I saw a great white throne, and him who sat on it, from whose face the earth and the heaven fled away. There was found no place for them. [12] And I saw the dead, both small and great, standing before the throne, and the books were opened. Another book was opened, which is the book of life. And the dead were judged by the things that were written in the books, according to their works. [13] And the sea gave up the dead which were in it. And death and Hades gave up the dead which were in them. And they were judged, every man according to his works.

The tribulation of the last days will lead directly to the end of the world. Verse 13 reiterates that the resurrection of those who are left in their graves after the rapture of the church and those who die in the subsequent tribulation will not occur until the end of the world. At that time, their evil deeds, which have been recorded because their names are not written in the book of life, will be revealed and judged. This is in contrast to the elect, who will be rewarded for their good deeds but pardoned of their wrongdoings.

Revelation 20:14-15

And death and Hades were thrown into the lake of fire. This is the second death, the lake of fire. [15] If anyone was not

Artist's depiction of the entrance to heaven
Lakeview Images / Shutterstock.com

REVELATION CHAPTER 21 – THE SEVENTH VISION

found written in the book of life, he was cast into the lake of fire.

To be thrown into the lake of fire is to be irreversibly destroyed. Death was irreversibly destroyed through the death and resurrection of Jesus Christ. There is no death for those who are in Christ Jesus. Hades, which is the temporary dwelling place of the dead, will be irreversibly destroyed because it will no longer exist after the dead are judged.

REVELATION 21:1

And I saw a new heaven and a new earth: for the first heaven and the first earth had passed away, and the sea was no more.

The New Heaven and the New Earth will be patterned after the present heaven and the present earth. There will be earth and sky, humans and animals, things to see and things to do; but everything in that plane of existence will be in a glorified form; that is, perfected for the glory of God (Rev. 5:13). The New World will be free of all the problems against which we strove in this world, such as hunger and thirst, pain and sickness, aging and death. Everything in the New World will be the way that God's faithful children were striving to make things in this world. That there was "no more sea" means that this perishable world will no longer exist.

REVELATION 21:2-7

And I saw the holy city, the new Jerusalem, coming down out of heaven from God, prepared like a bride adorned for her husband. [3] And I heard a loud voice out of heaven saying, Behold, the tabernacle of God is with men; he will dwell with them, and they will be his people, and He will be their God. [4] And He will wipe away every tear from their eyes. And death will be no more; neither will there be mourning, nor suffering, nor pain any more. For the former things have passed away. [5] And He who sat on the throne said, Behold, I make all things new. Then He said, Write; for these words of God are faithful and true. [6] Then He said to me, I am the Alpha and the Omega, the beginning and the end. To him who is thirsty I will freely give of the fountain of living water. [7] He who overcomes shall inherit these things; and I will be his God, and he will be my son.

The City of God in heaven is referred to as "the New Jerusalem" because it is the glorified form of the city that on earth was the place of God's chosen people—the Jews. The Good News is that the City of God is now open to everyone. After the fall of Adam, humankind was driven out of paradise; but humankind has been redeemed by the New Adam—Jesus Christ. All those who obediently trust in Him are being prepared like a bride for the bridegroom (Matt. 25:1). In the New World, the saved will not be separated from God because they will forever dwell physically in His kingdom. There will be no pain, sorrow, suffering, temptation, sin, or death in heaven because the body we now have, which is carnal, will be made spiritual. As such, it will be free of the vulnerability that leads to fear, anger, pride, competition, and all the other sins. Hence, all the temptations that we experience in this world will be gone, never to return again, and we will have open access to "fountains of living water," which is the tree of life referred to in Genesis 2:9.

The Rapture of People out of the world - Illustration

Benjamin Haas / Shutterstock.com

Revelation 21:8

But as for the cowardly, the unbelieving, the sinful, the abominable, the murderers, and those who commit adultery, and sorcerers, and idolaters, and all liars; their portion shall be in the lake that burns with fire and sulfur, which is the second death.

Hell will be established as a dwelling place for the damned. The "second death" is eternal damnation. What will make hell so much more unbearable and, conversely, heaven so much more glorious than anything we have experienced in this life is that the senses of the soul will no longer be subdued by the limitations of the physical eyes, physical ears, and other sensory organs. Also, apart from the earthly body, the depraved mind will not be able to ignore painful emotions through such defenses as denial, repression, sleep, and various chemical and physical distractions.

Revelation 21:9-16

And one of the seven angels who had the seven bowls full of the seven last plagues came and talked to me and said, Come, I will show you the bride, the wife of the Lamb. [10] And he carried me away in the Spirit to a great and high mountain, and showed me the holy city, the new Jerusalem, coming down out of heaven from God, [11] having the glory of God, radiating a brilliant light, shimmering as a jasper stone, clear as crystal. [12] And it had a great and high wall with twelve gates, and names were inscribed thereon, which are the names of the twelve tribes of the children of Israel; and at the gates, twelve angels. [13] On the east were three gates; on the north were three gates; on the south were three gates; and on the west were three gates. [14] And the wall of the city had twelve foundations, and on them were written the names of the twelve Apostles of the Lamb. [15] And he who talked to me had for a measuring rod a golden reed to measure the city, its gates, and its walls. [16] The city was laid four square, its length the same as its width. And he measured the city with the reed, twelve thousand stadia; it length, width, and height are equal.

The Lord reveals to Saint John that the New Jerusalem will be patterned after the earthly Jerusalem just as the New Heaven and the New Earth will be patterned after the present heaven and earth. Historically, Jerusalem was built in the shape of a cube and had twelve entrances or "gates." The New Jerusalem will have the same basic architecture. In reality, the world as we know it is patterned after God's heavenly kingdom.

Revelation 21:17

And he measured the wall thereof, a hundred and forty-four cubits, by the measure of a man, that is, of the angel.

"According to the measure of a man" means, in terms of human anatomy. In the biblical days, measurements were based on the size of body parts. The "cubit" was originally the length of a forearm, measured from the elbow to the fingertips, and the "span" was the distance from the tip of the thumb to the tip of the little finger when spread apart. In the book of Ezekiel we read, "The cubit is a cubit and a hand breadth" (Eze. 43:13). Over time, these became standardized to more consistent lengths. Prior to that, however, the exact length varied from place to place. For example, the Hebrew cubit was longer than the Egyptian cubit. On average, the cubit was

Gate of heaven
Christina Georgieva / Shutterstock.com

approximately forty-eight centimeters, and the span was approximately twenty-four centimeters (half a cubit). Genesis 6:15 tells us that the length of Noah's ark was three hundred cubits, which would equate to approximately four hundred and seventy-two feet (the length of an average city block). Then again, after the people were divided at the Tower of Babel, different cultures adopted different measurements. Thus, we cannot precisely translate the measurements that are given in the book of Revelation, which was written long after the days of Noah and Nimrod. Nonetheless, if we were to use approximations, the size of each dimension of the Holy City, being 12,000 furlongs (about an eighth of a mile), would equate to about fifteen hundred miles in length, width, and height. That means the city would span across most of the United States and rise far above the clouds.

REVELATION 21:18-20

The wall was made of jasper, and the city itself, of pure gold, resembling clear glass. [19] And the foundations of the city's wall were adorned with all kinds of precious stones. The first foundation was jasper; the second, sapphire; the third, chalcedony; the fourth, emerald; [20] the fifth, sardonyx; the sixth, sardius; the seventh, chrysolite; the eighth, beryl; the ninth, topaz; the tenth, chrysoprasus; the eleventh, jacinth; and the twelfth, amethyst.

The various stones described here represent the precious works of those who labored for the kingdom of Heaven. Each stone represents a different kind of work, whether it be preaching, teaching, healing, or some other kind of work in obedience to God. Numerous persons from around who have had a glimpse of the hereafter have corroborated the writings of Saint John.

REVELATION 21:21-25

The twelve gates were twelve pearls; each one of the gates was made of one pearl. And the great street of the city was of pure gold, as it were transparent glass. [22] I saw no temple therein, for the LORD God Almighty and the Lamb are its temple. [23] The city has no need of the sun to shine, neither of the moon to give its light, for the glory of God is the light of it, and its lamp is the Lamb. [24] And the nations of those who are saved shall walk in the light of it; and the kings of the earth shall bring their glory and honor into it. [25] Its gates will in no way be shut by day, for there will be no night there.

The light of the sun and moon are needed to illuminate our physical world, but they will not be needed to illuminate the New World because the Spirit of God will be its Light. In 1 John 5 we read, "...God is light, and in Him there is no darkness at all." In our present world the sun is symbolic of God and life, and the night is symbolic of death and destruction. We see both every day as a reminder that we must choose between the two. Those who choose the light will never again see darkness, and those who choose darkness will never again see the light (Jude 1:13). Jesus Christ is the Light, and His light is visible only to those who choose Him. Also, spiritual light is far brighter than physical light, and this is for two reasons. First, Spiritual light is love itself, which is the brightest and purest of lights. It is the uncreated light of God. Second, our bodies in the New World will be different than our bodies in this world. Here, we rely on the retina of the eye to see. This sense organ has to translate the energy of light into electrical signals that the brain can send to the mind. If the light is too bright it will become uncomfortable and could even damage the retina. The same is true of our hearing and other senses. Hence, our ability to experience this

The Holy Face of Jesus

world is limited by the transduction capabilities of our physical sense organs.

This limitation will not exist in the New World because we will see God's heavenly kingdom through the lens of the Holy Spirit. The resurrected body will not have sense organs that filter out information; instead, it will perceive everything as it truly is. Hence, colors will be sharper and more vivid; sounds will be sweeter and more harmonious; and the world will be filled with a glorious light because the light of the New World will be the Light of God's infinite love. Jesus said, "I am the light of the world" (John 8:12). This is not a symbolic statement. In the New World, God's love will literally illuminate all things just as the sun illuminates all things in this world. In truth, the light of God's love illuminates our present world also, but it is hidden from our human nature until we are born again spiritually. To be born again, we must receive the Holy Spirit. Only through the power of the Holy Spirit, which we receive when we surrender our lives to God, can we see God's heavenly light. In a sense, the Holy Spirit gives us the ability to see heavenly things in the same way that wearing a pair of 3-D glasses allows us to see the special effects in a 3-D movie. Apart from the Holy Spirit, we cannot see God's heavenly kingdom because it is illuminated by God's uncreated light. Jesus said, "Unless a man be born again, he cannot see the kingdom of God" (John 3:3).

In the eyes of God, the "king's of the earth" (vs. 24) are not those who have political authority over people but, rather, those who walk in obedience to God. They are kings of the earth in the sense that God blesses them with favor that no amount of money, talent, or intelligence can acquire. Jesus said, "Blessed are the meek, for they shall inherit the earth" (Matt. 5:5). He also said, "Seek first the kingdom of God and his righteousness; and all these things shall be added unto you" (Matt. 6:33).

REVELATION 21:26
And they shall bring the glory and honor of the nations into it.

When we behave honorably, we bring glory to all, and when we behave dishonorably, we bring dishonor to all. The "glory and the honor of the nations" are those who faithfully serve God on earth and, in so doing, bring glory to God and to the human race as a whole.

REVELATION 21:27
And in no way will anything profane enter into it, or one who causes an abomination or makes a lie, but only those whose names are written in the Lamb's book of life.

There never was nor ever can be any corruption in heaven else it would not be heaven. Again, the war that Saint John saw "in heaven" describes where he saw the vision. Saint John received the vision from above; hence, he describes the events as having taken place in heaven. However, that is not necessarily where the events actually occurred. By way of analogy, if I said that I saw a news report on television, that would not necessarily mean that the events took place inside the television set or in the news room. What the Apostle saw was symbolic; it was a "sign" of the spiritual battle that was occurring and would continue to occur on earth (Rev. 15:1). Also, angels could not literally sin because their bodies, being spiritual, are not subject to the temptations of the flesh. Pride, which is what some translators of the Bible believe the "fallen angels" were guilty of, stems from the vulnerability of the flesh. Knowing that our bodies are weak, we fear injury, sickness, and, ultimately, death. Pride is a defense against these fears. Instead of humbly relying upon God, we unconsciously tell ourselves that we are invincible. Having been lulled into this deception by their earthly power and position, many kings and leaders thoughtful history demanded strict submission of the people, and some even went so far as to proclaim themselves Gods on earth.

Picture of heaven on the pages of the Holy Bible

Amanda Carden / Shutterstock.com

Revelation 22:1-3

And he showed me a pure river of water of life, clear as crystal, proceeding out of the throne of God and of the Lamb. [2] And in the midst of the great street of the city, on either side of the river, was the tree of life, which bore twelve kinds of fruits, yielding its fruit each month. The leaves of the tree were for the healing of the nations. [3] And that which withers shall whither no more, but the throne of God and of the Lamb shall be in it; and his servants shall serve him.

Here is a picture of the "tree of life," which Jesus promised to those who do the will of the Father. The tree of life represents eternal life in our LORD and Savior Jesus Christ. Jesus Christ is the One through whom the world was created, and He is the One in whom we have true life—eternal life. The "twelve manner of fruits" are the blessings that came from the teachings of the twelve Apostles, and the leaves of the tree represent the spiritual healing that those teachings impart. In the Near East, the leaves of some trees were considered sacred, and some were used medicinally.

Revelation 22:4

And they will see his face, and his name will be on their foreheads.

Our LORD and Savior Jesus Christ will sit on the throne of God, and we shall see Him face to face. That His name will be "written on their foreheads" is an idiomatic expression that means that they will have the mind of Christ. As true believers, they had become entirely faithful and committed to the LORD, just as Jesus was faithful and committed to God.

Revelation 22:5-6

And there shall be no night there; nor need of candle, nor light of the sun, for the glory of God shines on them: and they shall reign for ever and ever. [6] And he said unto me, These sayings are faithful and true: and the LORD God of the holy prophets sent his angel to show unto his servants the things which must soon come to pass.

These verses are essentially a repetition of Rev. 21:23-25.

Revelation 22:7

Behold, I am coming quickly. Blessed is he who keeps the words of the prophecy of this book.

"Behold, I am coming quickly" means, I am coming on a day and at an hour that you least expect. Jesus told His disciples that He would return like a thief in the night, which is to say, He would catch people off guard (Matt. 24:43; Luke 12:39). We live in the eternal present, and so when something happens, it always seems to come upon us suddenly... unexpectedly. Also, life is short, and so whether we meet the Lord when he returns to this world or when we die, it will seem to catch us by surprise.

Revelation 22:8-9

Now I, John, am the one who heard and saw these things. And when I had heard and seen them, I fell down to worship before the feet of the angel who had shown me these things. [9] And he said to me, Do not do that; I am a fellow bondservant with you and with your brothers, the prophets, and with those who keep the words of this book. Worship God.

Jesus Christ looks at the South China sea. The view from the shoulder of the giant statue of Christ in Vung Tau, Vietnam

Karasev Victor / Shutterstock.com

Angels and saints are to be respected but not worshiped. If we include them in our prayers, it should be to humbly request their intercession. Only God is to be worshiped.

REVELATION 22:10

Then he said to me, Do not seal up the words of the prophecy of this book, for the time is at hand.

Saint John was to share his visions with his fellow believers and with all mankind. That is why he reduced his visions to writing. This also means that we are to study the book of Revelation and meditate on the prophecies therein, for these things will soon come to pass. The LORD is coming soon!

REVELATION 22:11

He who acts unjustly will continue to act unjustly; he who is filthy will continue to be filthy. And he who is righteous, let him continue to be righteousness; and he who is holy, let him continue to be holy.

The Revelator is not being told here that the unjust should remain unjust or that those who do wrong should continue to do wrong. Rather, he is being told that some people will persist in their ways right up until the end of their lives. At the same time, those who are on the path of righteousness are encouraged to remain on the path of righteousness. This is another reminder that the LORD will return at a time when we least expect; and when He does, there may not be any time to change our ways or repent of our wrongdoings. Practically speaking, this warning applies to all generations because even those who die before the LORD returns will meet Him; and when they do, the time to change their ways will have passed. Saint Paul wrote, "...to be absent from the body (is) to be present with the LORD" (2 Cor. 5:8). Therefore, it behooves us to prepare ourselves now even if we do not believe that the LORD will return during our lifetime.

REVELATION 22:12

Behold, I am coming soon, and my reward is with me, to repay every man according to his work.

Jesus will reward each of us according to our works; the saved will be rewarded for the good deeds they did in obedience to God, and the unsaved will be punished for the evils they did in disobedience to God. There will be no eternal rewards for the damned because no deed is considered good unless it is done in obedience to God and in the Spirit of God; that is, through the Holy Spirit, who is given to us by the LORD. Jesus said, "I am the vine, ye are the branches: He that abides in me, and I in him, the same brings forth much fruit: for without me you can do nothing" (John 15:5; Mark 10:8). Unless we give our lives to Jesus Christ, we can do nothing good by God's standard. Even so-called "good deeds" done apart from the Holy Spirit are done with the wrong spirit (wrong attitude), at the wrong time, and in the wrong way; hence, they are unacceptable to God. As for the wrongdoings of the saved, they will be washed away by the blood of Jesus Christ.

REVELATION 22:13-14

I am the Alpha and the Omega, the first and the last, the beginning and the end. [14] Blessed are those who keep his commandments, that they may have the right to the tree of life, and may enter through the gates into the city.

Through their disobedience to God, Adam and Eve lost access to the tree of life (vs. Gen. 3:24). The tree of life is the knowledge of God's love for us.

*Artist's depiction of God the Father looking down on creation,
Cima da Conegliano, c 1510-1517*

Courtesy of Wikipedia

When we lose sight of God's love, we naturally become disobedient to Him. Conversely, obedience to God is evidence of our faith in Him. Hence, obedience to God brings us back to the tree of life (1 John 2:5).

REVELATION 22:15

For outside are the ungodly, the sorcerers, the sexually immoral, the murderers, the idolaters, and everyone who loves and practices falsehood.

The evildoers cannot see God's light or His kingdom because they refuse to accept the Holy Spirit. Unless they have a change of heart while they are still alive in the flesh, they will die in their sins. Jesus repeatedly warned about the consequences of dying in our sins (John 8:24). This verse also refers back to 1 Cor. 6:9-10, in which we are told that "The unrighteous shall not inherit the kingdom of God...neither fornicators, nor idolaters, nor adulterers, nor effeminate, nor abusers of themselves with mankind, nor thieves, nor covetous, nor drunkards, nor revilers, nor extortioners, shall inherit the kingdom of God."

REVELATION 22:16

I, Jesus, have sent my angel to testify to you these things for the churches. I am the root and the offspring of David; the bright and morning star.

Jesus is the brightest star of heaven because He is the Light of the world.

REVELATION 22:17

The Spirit and the bride say, Come. And let him who hears say, Come. And he who is thirsty, let him come. And whoever will, let him freely take of the water of life.

The "water of life" symbolizes unity, peace, and abundance. Though all of us were created to live in peace and tranquility, they are scarce in this troubled world. Water is used figuratively because water was scarce in the land where the events of the Bible took place.

REVELATION 22:18-21

I testify to every man who hears the words of the prophecy of this book, If any man shall add to them, God shall add to him the plagues which are written in this book; [19] and if any man shall take away from the words of the prophesy of this book, God shall take away his portion of the tree of life, and from the holy city, and from the things which are written in this book. [20] He who testifies these things says, Surely I am coming soon. Amen. Come, LORD Jesus. [21] The grace of our LORD Jesus Christ be with all of you, all you holy ones. Amen.

The word of God is sacred, unchangeable, and timeless because it is the eternal truth. Anyone who would try to change it would be working against God. This is also a call to bear witness to the truth honestly, faithfully, and in obedience to the Holy Spirit. Amen+

Illuminated Manuscript, 13th century
Courtesy of Wikipedia

Concluding Comment

The seven prophetic visions that Saint John received correspond to the seven seals of the book of Revelation (Rev. 5:1). They are the contents of the book held by the One who sits on the throne of God. They were written to the seven elders, who are the seven angels, the seven stars, the seven lamps, the seven golden candlesticks, which are the seven churches named at the beginning of the book of Revelation. The angels who convey the visions are the seven spirits of God who have seven eyes, seven trumpets, and seven vials of wrath that will be poured out onto the earth. The seven seals also refer to the distinctions in detail, perspective, and symbolism that we see in Saint John's seven visions.

When we read the book of Revelation as seven parallel visions rather than one continuous sequence of events, the prophesy becomes surprisingly easy to interpret. With the exception of the sixth vision, which excludes the events leading up to the return of Jesus Christ, each of the seven visions describe the same prophetic events. Equally important, the sequence of the events is precisely the same in each of the visions. In each (with the exception of the sixth vision) we see the spiritual battle between good and evil beginning with the immaculate conception of Jesus Christ and ending with the rapture of the church. At the conclusion of the church age or "thousand-year reign of Christ," we see the wrath of God poured out upon those who remain on earth after the rapture.

Those who are left behind must not only bear God's wrath, but they must also bear the unrestrained wrath of each other because all the peacemakers will be gone. This hellish experience is symbolized by the escape of the devil from the bottomless pit for a short time (Rev. 20:3). The devil's brief reign of terror will be brought to an end by the fiery transformation of the universe as we know it (2 Peter 3:10-12). The devil and his angels, which symbolize all the evils of the world, will be cast into the lake of fire, and the New Heaven and the New Earth will be established (Rev. 19:20; 212:1).

The Revelation of Saint John describes a first resurrection that begins with Jesus Christ and is followed immediately by the resurrection of His most faithful followers (Acts 26:23; Rev. 14:4). Then, in an ongoing process, all those who live their lives wholly dedicated to God will likewise be resurrected immediately after they die. This is the "first resurrection." We

Saint John Receives His Revelation, Saint-Sever Beatus, 11th century
Courtesy of Wikipedia

know that this is a bodily resurrection because Saint Matthew tells us that the bodies of many of the Lord's faithful followers came out of their graves and went into the Holy City immediately after the resurrection of Jesus (Matt. 27:52-53). Also, the word "resurrection," as it is used in the Bible, does not refer to a spiritual event but, rather, an anatomical one. It refers to the rejoining of the spiritual body to an imperishable form of one's earthly body. Hence, like Jesus, those in the first resurrection have already been reunited with their physical bodies. The second resurrection, which chronologically refers to the resurrection of the rest of the faithful departed and to the elect who are still alive, will occur at the Lord's second coming. These blessed souls will meet the Lord in the air and follow Him to their heavenly home.

After that dramatic event, those left behind on earth will begin to suffer the natural consequences of their unrestrained and unforgiven sins. After a short time, their tribulation on earth will be brought to an end by a fiery transformation of the world as we know it (2 Peter 3:10). Immediately after that, all those who died in the tribulation and all those who were left in their graves during the rapture of the church will be resurrected and called to judgment.

The New Heaven and the New Earth will a glorified form of the present heaven and the present earth; that is, perfected. Every human being will have a spiritual body and a physical body just as we have now; but the physical body will be indestructible just as the New World will be, and it will have a spiritual nature rather than a carnal nature. The saved will dwell in a world of everlasting peace and love, while the damned will be eternally punished in body and spirit for the evils they committed on earth (Matt. 5:29).

The Lord's message is simple and certain. May all of us have the good sense to prepare ourselves for what will surely come. Amen+

+ + +

About the Author

MICHAEL R. BINDER, M.D. was born in Chicago, Illinois. He was raised in a home where he learned to pray from an early age and where trusting in God was a part of his daily life. From his childhood, he was drawn to the Scriptures, learning to read from a children's Bible and finding inspiration in the lives of the saints.

At the age of eighteen, he began premedical studies at the University of California, Los Angeles, where, by divine providence, he met Drs. Michael and Kathleen McCann, two university professors who lovingly nurtured his study of medicine and spirituality. In addition to his premedical studies, Dr. Binder served as a lay minister at the UCLA Medical Center.

In 1984 he graduated from the University of California and began medical school at Creighton University, where, in addition to his medical studies, he continued to serve as a lay minister. In 1988 he received his doctorate in medicine from the University of Chicago, Pritzker School of Medicine. From there he went on to specialize in the field of psychiatry, through which he gained a deeper understanding of the relationship between the mind, body, and spirit.

After several years in practice, Dr. Binder began to find that there were some patients who he could not successfully treat. Unwilling to give up on these treatment-resistant patients, he began to pray for them and ask God for help in healing them. The LORD answered by calling him back to the Bible, a spiritual journey that led to the healing of himself and some of his most difficult patients.

After ten years of intensive Bible study, Dr. Binder was inspired to write *Images of Heaven*, a commentary on the Holy Bible through the lens of science. Writing at a pace of more than forty hours per week during the first five years, the book took more than thirteen years to complete, hampered mainly by difficulties interpreting the book of Revelation. After much research, prayer, and fasting, the LORD opened the doctor's mind to the interpretation of Saint John's visions, and both the completion of *Images of Heaven* and the writing of *Revelation Revealed* became possible.

Other Books By This Author

All of Dr. Binder's books are available through the Binder Foundation. To learn more or to place an order, please visit www.binderfoundation.com

Miracles: Ask and Ye Shall Receive

Miracles is a book of personal memoirs that recounts the acts of God in the life of Dr. Michael Binder, a physician and scientist, who has witnessed the loving hand of God through faith time and again. Packed with more than one hundred miracles, this inspirational work describes the experiences of the doctor himself, which are presented with the historical accuracy and attention to detail that one would expect from a clinical scientist. Those who believe in God will be strengthened by this book; those who are uncertain will be inspired; and those who do not believe will be challenged to take the leap of faith that opens the door to heaven on earth.

Images of Heaven: A Book of Love, Wisdom & Truth

This unique work is a study of the Holy Bible through the lens of science. Based on the most authentic complete Bible manuscripts in existence, Dr. Michael Binder combines his medical training and experience as a psychiatrist with the knowledge and insights of world-renown Bible scholar Dr. George M. Lamsa to help you understand the entire Bible, from the book of Genesis to the book of Revelation, in the language of our modern culture and times.

Am I Depressed Or Am I Bipolar?

This groundbreaking book is intended to help readers understand psychiatric disorders from an anatomical, psychological, and spiritual perspective with an emphasis on helping the reader make the distinction between classic unipolar depression and bipolar disorder. Drawing on years of clinical experience and intensive personal study, board-certified psychiatrist Dr. Michael Binder unveils the full anatomy of the cognitive-emotional system and uses numerous case examples to familiarize the reader with the various forms that mood disorders can take. Along with that, he discusses the fastest, safest, and most continuously effective way to treat them.

Mysteries of the Mind: Two Astonishing Articles that Solve the Mystery

Despite centuries of scientific study and philosophical debate, the structure, function, and seemingly unlimited potential of the human mind continue to be a mystery. The brain has been studied anatomically, chemically, and physiologically, yet the medical field is still no closer to understanding the mind than it was a century ago. That's because most of the astounding abilities that belong to the mind have mistakenly been attributed to the brain. The brain is merely a computer in the head that records, integrates, and plays back information that it receives from the mind and the body.

The two articles presented in this book, written by the neuropsychiatrist who published the first comprehensive psychophysiological hypothesis of psychiatric disorders, provide clinical, anatomical, and electrophysiological evidence that the mind and the brain are distinctly different but tightly integrated entities that continuously interact with each other as they process information from the environment, govern the body, and encode memories. In the first article, the precise location of the mind deep within the brain is identified, and its dynamic relationship with the brain is used to explain a number of heretofore inexplicable phenomena including learning, memory, unconscious thought, abnormal thought, dissociative states, and out-of-body experiences. In the second article, the mind-brain relationship is used to explain near-death experiences and to provide a precise definition for the mysterious divide between life and death.

Although scientifically-sound in their logic, these articles transcend science because they incorporate that which cannot be seen with the eye or analyzed with physical instrumentation; they incorporate the spiritual element or "soul" of a human being. From this more anatomically and functionally compete perspective, they supply answers to some of the most challenging questions in the fields of psychological, psychiatry, and neurology.

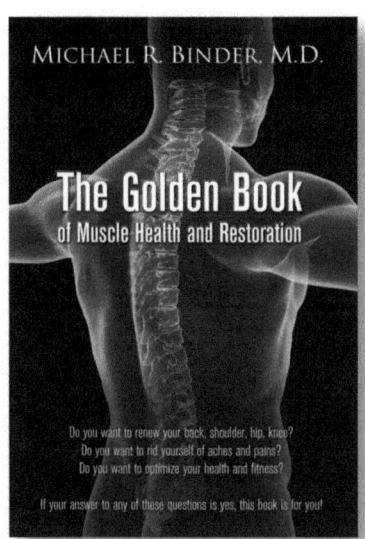

The Golden Book of Muscle Health and Restoration

The Golden Book is a revolutionary look at the hidden cause of chronic musculoskeletal pain and the most effective way to treat it.

Based on his own struggles with chronic pain and the brilliant work of Dr. Thomas Griner, Dr. Michael Binder addresses the little-known but extremely common problem of *hypertonic muscle spasm*. In this life-changing book, you will discover how hypertonic spasm develops, how it causes symptoms, and, if you are already suffering from its ill effects, what to do to get out of pain and stay out of pain without the need for drugs, injections, or surgery. We're talking about truths that are destined to revolutionize orthopedic medicine, physical rehabilitation, and the fitness world! So if you want to preserve the vitality of your muscles and get the most out of them; or, conversely, if you have ever thrown out your back, developed chronic joint pain, or experienced frightening symptoms like urinary incontinence or nerve irritation down an arm or leg, this book is for you!

The Racing Mind: Brave New Insights Untangle the Ancient Mystery of Mental Illness

The Racing Mind is a revolutionary look at mental illness that presents the first comprehensive psychophysiological hypothesis of psychiatric disorders. Based on the simple premise that psychiatric symptoms are caused by pathological hyperactivity of symptom-related circuits in the brain, the new hypothesis streamlines treatment and circumvents the need for stigmatizing diagnoses.

According to the multi-circuit neuronal hyperexcitability hypothesis, the brain hyperactivity that drives psychiatric symptoms is caused by mental and emotional stress superimposed upon a hyper-reactivity or "hyperexcitability" of the neurological system. Without treatment, affected persons have a tendency to overanalyze and overdramatize everything in their lives, thus leading to the various signs and symptoms that characterize psychiatric and substance use disorders. Neuronal hyperexcitability also places affected persons at increased risk for developing any of a wide range of chronic medical conditions, including high blood pressure, diabetes, heart disease, autoimmune disease, cancer, and dementia. The recognition of this is revolutionizing the way that psychiatric symptoms are conceptualized. It is changing them from being viewed as signs of mental and emotional weakness to early warning signs of a neurophysiological abnormality that is at the root of virtually every chronic disease. Beyond opening up new vistas in preventive medicine, these transformative insights have catapulted the author's success rate in treating mental illness from around 30% to nearly 100% and reduced the average time to symptom-reduction from about six months to six days!!

The Racing Mind is a must-read for any clinician, patient, or researcher who is serious about getting to the root of mental illness, restoring hope, and reducing the long-held stigma of this highly common but gravely misunderstood group of disorders.

www.ingramcontent.com/pod-product-compliance
Lightning Source LLC
Chambersburg PA
CBHW040846100426
42812CB00014B/2618